Formal Medieval Combat and Performance

Mark Geldof

Formal Medieval Combat and Performance

The Woodville-Burgundy *Emprise* of 1467

Mark Geldof
REGINA, SK, Canada

ISBN 978-3-031-91909-1   ISBN 978-3-031-91910-7 (eBook)
https://doi.org/10.1007/978-3-031-91910-7

© The Editor(s) (if applicable) and The Author(s), under exclusive license to Springer Nature Switzerland AG 2025

This work is subject to copyright. All rights are solely and exclusively licensed by the Publisher, whether the whole or part of the material is concerned, specifically the rights of translation, reprinting, reuse of illustrations, recitation, broadcasting, reproduction on microfilms or in any other physical way, and transmission or information storage and retrieval, electronic adaptation, computer software, or by similar or dissimilar methodology now known or hereafter developed.

The use of general descriptive names, registered names, trademarks, service marks, etc. in this publication does not imply, even in the absence of a specific statement, that such names are exempt from the relevant protective laws and regulations and therefore free for general use.

The publisher, the authors and the editors are safe to assume that the advice and information in this book are believed to be true and accurate at the date of publication. Neither the publisher nor the authors or the editors give a warranty, expressed or implied, with respect to the material contained herein or for any errors or omissions that may have been made. The publisher remains neutral with regard to jurisdictional claims in published maps and institutional affiliations.

This Palgrave Macmillan imprint is published by the registered company Springer Nature Switzerland AG.

The registered company address is: Gewerbestrasse 11, 6330 Cham, Switzerland

If disposing of this product, please recycle the paper.

Preface

Steven Muhlberger's 2011 lecture at the International Congress of Medieval Studies, Kalamazoo, addressed the challenges period sources posed for the study of military biography. Some sources resisted analysis, but persistence and time often yielded results. Therefore, Muhlberger advised that "old sources deserve a new look every once and a while [...] once a century is about right."[1] This was said in reference to one of the more frustrating sources for the study of medieval combat, namely, the series of eye-witness accounts of the arranged combat between Anthony Woodville, Lord Scales, and Antoine de Bourgogne, commonly called The Bastard of Burgundy (the illegitimate son of Philip the Good).[2] The men fought each other over two summer days at Smithfield, London: the first day on horseback and the second day on foot.[3] Sydney Anglo produced one of the few detailed studies of the episode and compared the two most detailed accounts but concluded that, for all their vivid language, neither

---

[1] Steven Muhlberger, 'Chivalry and Military Biography in the Later Middle Ages: The Chronicle of the Good Duke Louis of Bourbon', *The Journal of Medieval Military History*, X (2012), p. 113, 115.

[2] In contrast to modern usage, the title of 'Bastard' here acknowledges the individual's noble blood, and there were several royal Bastards of Britany and Orléans. See a discussion of this usage in Helen Matthews, *The Legitimacy of Bastards: The Place of Illegitimate Children in Later Medieval England* (Pen and Sword, 2019).

[3] The family name is found spelled Wydville, Wideville, and Wodevile, among others, but is here given as 'Woodville' throughout.

seemed to agree in detail, and on some points they "flatly contradicted" each other.[4] Anyone hoping to reconstruct a combat, blow-by-blow, would give up in frustration when confronted with these accounts. And this was certainly Muhlberger's experience. However, his point was that there were plenty of things one could still learn from even contradictory sources. As our understanding of the broader social and political influences on late medieval chivalric culture has increased, so too has our capacity to find new meaning in old sources. As John Morrill explained, "[E]very historian believes but struggles to prove that knowledge of the past helps us to understand the present. It is so much easier to see how experience of the present helps us to understand the past."[5] Thus, the value of returning to old sources, once dismissed as fatally flawed.

The present collection of all contemporary and near-contemporary accounts of the Woodville-Burgundy emprise was assembled with this goal of asking new questions of old sources. None of these accounts are new to historians, but few of them are easily accessible and only even fewer are available in English translation. Nowhere have all (or even most) of the accounts appeared together in a way that would permit closer comparison. While it must be acknowledged that a more formal edition of the following accounts, with orthographic notation and, where possible, facing-page translations and transcriptions would be valuable, the scope of the present study is simply to provide readable modern editions of the accounts for reference and comparison. The introduction provides historical contexts for the concept of the pas d'arms and the emprise—late medieval forms of the arranged combats involving Europe's martial elites. It also provides more specific contexts for the Woodville-Burgundy emprise and the social, political, and literary contexts in which the event took place. Many questions are posed of the sources, but not all of them can be answered here. Instead, this is an exercise in the collection and presentation of a body of historical material, as a tool for working on those questions and discovering new ones, that are still worth asking.

---

[4] Muhlberger, "Chivalry and Military Biography," p. 114. The study is S. Anglo, 'Anglo-Burgundian Feats of Arms: Smithfield, June 1467', *Guildhall Miscellany*, 2.1 (1965), pp. 271–83.

[5] John Morrill, 'Thinking About the New British History', in *British Political Thought in History, Literature and Theory, 1500–1800*, ed. by David Armitage (CUP, 2006), p. 23.

Thanks are due to Dr. Muhlberger for encouraging this project; to my partner Zena Charowsky for her patience in sharing her space with it; and to Carly Silver and the staff at Palgrave Macmillan for guiding this project into print. I hope this gives students and scholars of this event a place to start more involved projects.

Regina, SK   Mark Geldof

Competing Interests

The author has no competing interests to declare that are relevant to the content of this manuscript.

Contents

1	**Introduction**	1
	The Emprise *of the Flower of* Souvenance	8
	After the Emprise	11
	Editorial Conventions	12
	Bibliography	12
2	**The Sources**	15
	Chester Herald	15
	Anonymous Burgundian	45
	Olivier de la Marche Mémoires	71
	Jehan de Wavrin's Chronicle	77
	Enguerrand de Monstrelet's Chronicle (Continuation)	78
	Gregory's Chronicle	79
	Cotton MS Vitellius A XVI	80
	Lambeth MS 306	81
	Howard's Chronicle	82
	The Great Chronicle of London	83
	Chronicle of Robert Fabyan	85
	Pseudo-Worcester	86
	Hall's Chronicle	86
	Bibliography	89
	Cumulative Bibliography	93
	Index	99

About the Author

Mark Geldof completed a D.Phil. at Merton College Oxford, UK, in 2018. He studied the shifting meanings of violence among late medieval and early modern English social elites. In addition to his history training, he holds degrees in English Literature and Library Science. Published work includes the history of martial pedagogy, text-production, and the earliest English fight-texts. He has written about the role of the archaeology of physical trauma in studies of violence. He has also edit two books on the history of modern firearms for Safar Publishing, from Ukraine.

ABBREVIATIONS[1]

AB   Anonymous Burgundian account (Utrecht, Hs 6b 9)
CH   the account of Chester Herald
Excerpta   S. Bentley, ed. Excerpta Historica: or Illustrations of English History (1831)
Leeds   Leeds, Royal Armouries RAR 00035 (manuscript copy of AB)
de la Marche Memoirs of Olivier de la Marche
Monstrelet   Chronicle continuation of Enguerrand de Monstrelet
Utrecht   Utrecht University Library ms 1117 / hs 6b9 (manuscript copy of AB)

[1] Common sources mentioned in the introduction and notes are cited in full, in the first instance but will use the following abbreviations thereafter.

CHAPTER 1

Introduction

Abstract The formal combat, arranged between Anthony Woodville, Lord Scales, and The Bastard of Burgundy in the summer of 1467 is one of the best documented of the late medieval forms of *emprise*, a form of chivalric theater fought with weapons of war before an international audience of nobles and social elites. While this particular event is familiar to scholars of European chivalry, the several accounts are rarely discussed in detail. This *emprise* permits a closer study of social structures, shared values and interests, and a common vocabulary of chivalric culture in the fifteenth century.

Keywords *Emprise* • Chivalry • Courtly culture • *Pas d'armes* • Formal combat

Formal combats in the medieval period pose problems for modern readers of history. The notion of potentially fatal combat as a form of play is difficult to fathom but so too is the idea that such performances were a respectable part of elite culture and a forum for dignified and honorable conduct. The staged combats of the early middle-ages were created largely as a means of improving skill in arms and building an *esprit des corps* among the martial elites. The social and cultural structure of Chivalry was constructed by, and for, these martial elites and the display of prowess was so important that the staged combat was considered nearly as important as warfare itself.[1] In later years, these combats increasingly acted as a means to perform before a noble audience who found in the tournament a new stage to display personal wealth and sophistication. Formal combats, and the social events surrounding them, grew into an extension of medieval court culture and diplomatic theater where combatants and non-combatants could participate in a wider, pan-European, performance of chivalric and romantic ideals. In turn, this changed the way formal combats were arranged and performed. The melee, fought over a large area and without any real audience, gave way to the smaller, more stage-managed events such as the *emprise*.[2]

The *emprise* was 'a chivalric exploit undertaken by a knight or squire who was therefore deemed to be its *entrepreneur*.'[3] The most popular form of *emprise* was the *pas d'armes* (passage of arms) which involved one or more knights who would issue a challenge to all commers (so long as they were of noble birth). These challenges could be fought by individuals or teams but usually took place between paired individuals rather than multiple combatants engaged in a melee.[4] This shift to the theatrical is often identified by later historians as 'the epitome of the end of Chivalry' because it seemed to abandon the practical military aspects in favor of spectacle.[5] While there remains some debate as to the centrality of martial skill in later tournaments, participation in them remained a dangerous activity and few concessions were made for the sake of safety, and sharp

---

[1] Writing in the fourteenth century, French knight Geoffroi de Charny considered deeds of arms performed at tournaments to be just below deeds performed in local wars in their degree of moral value as a reflection of chivalric prowess (Richard W. Kaeuper and Elspeth Kennedy, *The Book of Chivalry of Geoffroi de Charny: Text, Context, and Translation*. (University of Pennsylvania Press, 1996), p. 87).

[2] On this transformation see Richard Barber and Juliet R. V. Barker, *Tournaments* (Boydell Press, 1989), pp. 13–47. See also Sébastien Nadot, *Rompez les lances! chevaliers et tournois au moyen âge* (Autrement, 2010), p. 115. The meaning of *emprise* in this context is often abstract but the translation of the term as an 'initiative' in the sense of an undertaking or vow, captures the intent fairly well, see Steven Muhlberger, *Deeds of Arms: Formal Combats in the Late Fourteenth Century* (Chivalry Bookshelf, 2005), p. 44. Nadot explains that the word was borrowed from a Castilian term referring to the negotiation of a difficult problem (Nadot, *Rompez*, p. 117).

[3] *Pas d'armes and Late Medieval Chivalry: A Casebook*, ed. by Rosalind Brown-Grant and Mario Damen (Liverpool University Press, 2025), p. 2.

[4] Ibid.

[5] H.N. MacCracken, "The Flower of *Souvenance*: A Moment in the Twilight of Chivalry." *The Swanee Review*, 20, no. 3 (1912), p. 366.

weapons remained a common feature.[6] Tournaments were also easily associated with political faction and intrigue that could threaten the established order.[7] The Christian Church abhorred the practice for various reasons, not least of which was the risk accepted by skilled combatants and leaders of men who were otherwise valuable to the Church in its defense.[8] There were secular arguments against the practice as well, and while the carefully stage-managed events of the fifteenth century were less destructive of local environments and took fewer lives from its participants, it was still seen as decadent and irresponsible.[9] But these critics could not compete with the rewards on offer to those who were able to pursue them.

One reason why we have so many accounts of the Woodville and Burgundy *emprise* is because these events held aspirational interest for members of the gentry and those who aspired to join the ranks of the martial elite. To that end there was enough demand for literary accounts of deeds of arms and the *emprise* that readers collected accounts in compendiums of heraldic and chivalric history. This created a literary genre that became its own force within the community of chivalry that it served.[10]

By the start of the fifteenth century, the region of Burgundy became the leader in the development of the *pas d'armes*.[11] Ornate and deeply symbolic aspects could be paired with involved and taxing endeavors. The *pas* held on an island across from the town of Chalon-sur-Saône, lasted more than a year, pitting its *entrepreneur*, Jacques de Lalaing (c.1421–53), against all challengers.[12] While spectacle grew in importance, combat remained an essential part of these events and participants ranged from

---

[6] This debate is discussed in Baker-Grant and Damen, pp. 12–16.

[7] They were often banned during the reign of King John and they were tightly restricted during Henry III's minority (Barber and Barker, *Tournaments*, pp. 29–30).

[8] The Church did not explicitly ban tournaments, as such, but did deny burial within church grounds to those were killed participating in them (Canon 14, 2nd Lateran Council, 1139: *Disciplinary Decrees of the General Councils*, ed. by H. J. Schroeder (B. Herder, 1937), p. 203).

[9] On clerical criticism of martial play, see Richard W. Kaeuper, *Holy Warriors: The Religious Ideology of Chivalry* (University of Pennsylvania Press, 2009), pp. 66–7.

[10] See Curt E Bühler, 'Sir John Paston's Grete Booke, a Fifteenth-Century "Best-Seller"', *Modern Language Notes*, 56.5 (1941), pp. 345–51.

[11] Mario Damen, 'Tournament Culture in the Low Countries and England', in *Contact and Exchange in Later Medieval Europe Essays in Honour of Malcolm Vale*, ed. by Hannah Skoda (Boydell & Brewer, 2012), pp. 247–66.

[12] Baker-Grant and Damen, pp. 152–3.

professional soldiers to members of the ruling royalty.[13] Because the *emprise* needed an audience for it to realize its full value as a means of earning renown and exhibiting prowess, these events were an ideal vehicle for informal networking and diplomacy. This was facilitated by the well organized and established community of heralds who had become a feature of martial diplomacy. Heralds were essential for recording and disseminating knowledge of chivalric deeds and that fame sustained the chivalric self.[14] In the early years of the reign of Edward IV, Burgundy became a politically and strategically important ally in the near-constant cycle of conflict between England and France and the remaining threat of the deposed Lancastrian faction of Henry VI. It is against the backdrop of this wider political situation that made modern historians of the period interested in the records of this particular combat.

Edward IV (1442–83) was, in 1465, reasonably secure on his throne with Henry VI (1421–71) in custody and his formidable Queen (Margaret of Anjou, 1430–82) in exile with the couple's only son, Edward (1453–71). Their few supporters were pushed into the Kingdom's fringes but were still a thorn in the new King's side. While they remained a credible threat to Edward's hold on power, he would need to cultivate friends, or at least reduce the number of enemies if he had any hope of leaving a viable dynasty to his children. The powerful Duchy of Burgundy represented a potential ally against French interests who were themselves often at odds with the French King, Louis XII. Duke Philip the Good (1396–1467) was a shrewd statesman and marriage ties with Burgundy had been considered for Edward himself, but his secret marriage to the widow, Elizabeth Woodville, in 1464, undermined several schemes for diplomatic marriages.[15] The Woodville family, however, provided Edward with a body of courtiers he was able to use in ways that circumvented pre-existing

[13] René of Anjou, duke of Anjou and James IV of Scotland fought in several events as *entrepenures* (ibid., pp. 28–30).

[14] Anthony Richard Wagner, *Heralds & Heraldry in the Middle Ages: An Inquiry into the Growth of the Armorial Function of Heralds*, 2nd ed. (Oxford University Press, 1956), pp. 12–40, 46–55. On the role of Heralds in warfare and the tournament, see Robert W. Jones, *Bloodied Banners: Martial Display on the Medieval Battlefield*, (Boydell Press, 2010).

[15] This is explored in detail in J. R. Lander, 'Marriage and Politics in the Fifteenth Century: The Nevilles and the Wydevilles', *Historical Research*, 36, no. 94 (1963), pp. 119–52. On Anthony Woodville's life, see Colin Richmond, 'Woodville [Wydeville], Anthony, Second Earl Rivers (c. 1440–1483), Magnate', *Oxford Dictionary of National Biography*, online ed. (2011). On the Woodville family, see recent work by Susan Higginbotham, *The Woodvilles: The Wars of the Roses and England's Most Infamous Family* (The History Press, 2013), and

factional conflicts or cliques, particularly in his more theatrical dealings with other powers. He made his father-in-law, Richard, Earl Rivers (1405–69) his Chamberlain and gave his eldest son, Anthony, Lord Scales, a prominent place amongst his closest attendants.[16]

Anthony Woodville was the Queen's eldest brother and neither he, nor his father, were strangers to Edward before he became King. The Woodvilles had supported Henry VI in 1459–61 and Father and son were both captured by dissident Yorkists during a raid on the port of Sandwich in January 1460. They were transported to Calais (at the time, firmly in the hands of the Richard, Earl of Warwick, the Duke of York's greatest supporter) where they were 'rated' by Warwick and young Edward, (at the time, Earl of March). Father and son were told they were promoted above their stations, lacking the nobility of blood of their captors. The senior Woodville had certainly built well on what he was born with, marrying Jacquetta of Luxembourg (c.1415–72) the widow of the Duke of Bedford, Henry VI's uncle.[17] Father and son were eventually freed and participated in the catastrophic battle of Towton (28–29 March 1461), where Anthony was wounded and thought killed.[18] Anthony also married well. Sometime before 1462 he married Elizabeth, daughter of the late Thomas, who brought her father's title and several properties to the union. This entitled Anthony to the status of Lord Scales.[19] A curious detail that is reproduced in the earliest accounts of the *emprise* is the habit of referring to Woodville

the most recent biography of Anthony Woodville by Danielle Burton, *Anthony Woodville: Sophisticate or Schemer?* (Amberley, 2024).

[16] Michael Hicks, 'Woodville [Wydeville], Richard, First Earl Rivers (d. 1469), Magnate', *Oxford Dictionary of National Biography*, online ed. (2011).

[17] Lucia Diaz Pascual, 'Jacquetta of Luxembourg, Duchess of Bedford and Lady Rivers (c. 1416-1472)', *The Ricardian*, 21 (2011): pp. 67–91.

[18] Recent work by Tim Sutherland argues that the initial contact between opposing forces at Ferrybridge, 28 March, and the larger battle at Towton on the 29th are one continuous encounter, rather than two discreet events, which accounts for the significantly higher casualties seen here (Tim Sutherland, 'Killing Time: Challenging the Common Perceptions of Three Medieval Conflicts—Ferrybridge, Dintingdale and Towton—'The Largest Battle on British Soil", *Journal of Conflict Archaeology*, 5.1 (2009), pp. 1–25).

On the capture of the Woodvilles at Sandwich, David Baldwin, (in *Elizabeth Woodville: Mother of the Princes in the Tower* (Stroud: Sutton, 2004), p. 8), speculates that they were freed following the Yorkist victory at Northampton in July that year, which is consistent with the attempts to mitigate tensions following the Yorkist capture of Henry VI. See also Higginbotham, p. 24.

[19] Elizabeth inherited the title through her father, Thomas, who was the 7th Lord Scales in that line, and was a friend and college of Richard, Earl Rivers. She died 1473 without having

as Lord Scales 'and of Newsells.' He is so styled in patent rolls from 1466 and it appears this was in reference to one of the manorial residences attached to the title, which was located near Barkway in Hertfordshire.[20] The difference in title fell out of use after 1467 as there was actually no need to distinguish him from any other 'Scales.' These advancements by the Woodville family, however, paled in comparison to the fortune shown after the marriage of Edward IV to Anthoney's sister Elizabeth. There was a practical reason for Edward's preferential treatment of the Woodville family, despite the irritation it caused the establishment. Their outsider status gave Edward a pool of loyal servants who were more intimately dependent on him for their ongoing success than were many of his noble supporters and this worked to counterbalance the ambitions of Edward's less trustworthy peers.[21]

Henry VI never had much interest in the spectacle of staged combats, and rarely witnessed them (and may never have participated in them), but his subjects felt differently. Edward came to the throne with a well-earned reputation as an energetic soldier and representation if Chivalry and he capitalized on that in his early years. Edward organized a tournament to follow his Queen's formal coronation on 27 May 1465, which involved several hundred combatants and a significant Burgundian contingent. This event took place around a month after the *emprise* was issued to Woodville by the Queen's ladies-in-waiting, as described in account of the Chester Herald (cited as **CH**, from here-on).[22]

By this time, Anthony had become one of Edwards favorite tournament companions and was building a reputation as a man of war and letters.[23] He was, therefore, a good candidate for this form of chivalric performance. The choice of Antoine, Count of Le Salle and La Roche, (1421–1504) and 'natural son' of the Duke of Burgundy was a natural choice for an opponent, from both a social and diplomatic perspective.

any children with Anthony (Lynda Pidgeon, 'Antony Wydevile, Lord Scales and Earl Rivers: Family, Friends and Affinity Part 2', *The Ricardian*, 16 (2006), pp. 1–3).
[20] The other manors were Middleton in Norfolk and Rivenhall, Essex (*Calendar of Patent Rolls [...] Edward IV, 1461-1467*, (Public Records Office: 1897), p. 533, 535).
[21] This had mixed benefits for the King: C. D. Ross, *Edward IV* (Yale, 1997), pp. 99–100.
[22] *Excerpta Historica: Or Illustrations of English History*, ed. by S. Bentley (S. Bentley, 1831), p. 200 (hereafter cited as *Excerpta*).
[23] Emma Levitt, 'Tiltyard Friendships and Bonds of Loyalty in the Reign of Edward IV, 1461-1483', in *Loyalty to the Monarchy in Late Medieval and Early Modern Britain, c.1400-1688*, ed. by Matthew Ward and Matthew Hefferan (Palgrave, 2020), pp. 22–3.

1 INTRODUCTION 7

Antoine was a close servant of his father and by 1465 had made an impressive career as a soldier and tournament performer.[24] Since Burgundy set the fashion for chivalric display at the time and the involvement of one of the Duchy's most celebrated representatives of chivalric culture would elevate the English *emprise* to an international spectacle. It also accommodated diplomatic interests Edward already had with Burgundy, particularly early negotiations to marry his sister Margaret to Philip the Good's son and heir, Charles, Count of Charlois.[25] While entirely coincidence that Woodville and Burgundy shared a first name, their shared literary and martial interests were consistent with their place in the social hierarchy and their proximity to the seats of power. Anthony would produce several translations of popular scholarly texts that informed the intellectual and moral world of late medieval chivalry and The Bastard of Burgundy was likewise a patron of the arts and was a key figure in what is often considered the golden age of Burgundian arts and letters.[26] This interest in the arts and fantastic literature also influenced the form that the *pas d'armes* and the *emprise* would take in Burgundy. Sometimes these expressions bordered on the absurd as when The Bastard appeared at the 1458 *Pas du Compagnon a' la Larme Blanche* on a platform 'mounted and armed in a cell that resembled a kind of chapel that could be carried' at La Quesnoy.[27]

The *emprise* of 1467 may have been the first meeting of Woodville and The Bastard, although the anonymous Burgundian account (hereafter cited as **AB**) mentions an abortive *emprise* in 1463 that would have seen three defenders, including the Bastard, fighting three challengers, one of whom was to be Anthony Woodville, who had already touched the *emprise* device.[28] Events intervened and the enterprise may not have been

---

[24] Richard Vaughan, *Philip the Good: The Apogee of Burgundy*, New ed (Boydell Press, 2002), pp. 134–5. By 1464 Antoine had even led a Burgundian contingent on crusade, although the project was abandoned before the Pope's forces reached their intended destination (ibid., p. 218).

[25] Levitt, pp. 23–4.

[26] On Anthony's academic interests see Omar Khalaf, 'Patronage, Print and the Education of the Gentry in Late Medieval England: The Case of Earl Rivers's Dicts and Sayings of the Philosophers', in *Current Issues in Medieval England*, ed. by L. Vazzosi (Peter Lang, 2021), pp. 46–58. On The Bastard as patron of the arts, see Vaughn, *Philip the Good*, p. 155.

[27] Brown-Grant and Damen, p. 197.

[28] This account survives in two manuscript copies. The copy in the collection of the Royal Armouries, Leeds (RAR 00035) is transcribed and translated in Ralph Dominic Moffat, 'The Medieval Tournament: Chivalry, Heraldry and Reality, an Edition and Analysis of Three Fifteenth-Century Tournament Manuscripts' (unpublished Ph.D., University of Leeds,

performed. A *pas* was planned for Bruges, in February, 1463, but no one attended.[29] It may reference the *pas* that took place in June 1463 in Brussels, but that event did go ahead as planned.[30] It was probably this missed opportunity that motivated the *emprise* of the flower of remembrance.

THE *EMPRISE* OF THE FLOWER OF *SOUVENANCE*

At the heart of the *emprise* were the conditions that the *entrepreneur* had to satisfy to earn his release (metaphorically and sometimes literally) from the burden of the challenge he had accepted. These conditions were articulated in a set of rules, called 'chapters' that sometimes told a dramatic tale with a moral lesson, although not always. The *emprise* given to Woodville is nothing more than for 'the worshipful reverence and help of our blessed savior Jesus Christ, of the glorious Virgin his mother, and Saint George, [the] very tutor and patron and cry of Englishmen, in augmentation of knighthood and recommendation of nobility, also for the glorious school and study of arms and for the courage,' according to **CH**. This pledge is given to Woodville in the form of a garter or collar (both terms are used) bearing an enameled pendant 'in the shape of a flower of *souvenance*,' which is a poetic reference to a forget-me-not. This object was initially tied to Woodville's thing ('closer to his heart, than his knee' **CH** tells us).[31] This is a symbolic and literal representation of the *emprise* and is sent with Chester Herald on his embassy to Burgundy, where it is presented to The Bastard who touches it, as part of the acceptance of the challenge. One may expect some additional symbolic reference to the flower, but other than its use as the *emprise* there is nothing about the chapters themselves that make anything of the act of remembrance. It is simply a framing device for the *emprise* itself.

The accounts of the *emprise* describe an involved process of planning the details of the challenge, the process of presenting the challenge, and its

---

2010). The second copy, from which the present edition was prepared is Utrecht University Library ms 1117 / hs 6b9.

[29] This was the *Pas de la Dame Inconnue*, organised by Pedro Vásquez de Saavedra (Brown-Grant and Damen, pp. 334–5).

[30] Ibid., pp. 410–11.

[31] This was a common feature of the *emprise* and acted in the same way that the shields or other stationary symbols used in the *pas d'armes* where challengers indicated their willingness to participate, by touching it with their hand or arms (Baker-Grant and Damen, p. 533).

rules to the chosen opponent, and a significant amount of travel. All of this was conducted in a public manner with the letters read before assembled courts, formal presentations before royalty, and the exchange of gifts. Initially the *emprise* was planned to occur in London, late in 1465 but Burgundian politics intervened, delaying the *emprise* until the summer of 1467. As it turned out, the timing of events meant that there was a much larger English audience than would have been available earlier. Parliament was summoned to Westminster for 3 June and Edward informally prorogued the meeting on the 10th to allow anyone who wished, to attend at Smithfield.[32] This also gave Edward ample time to meet with the Burgundian party and to entertain them afterwards.

It is in this part of the accounts that we find the first contradictions between **CH** and **AB** in that the Burgundian account places the Bastard's arrival in London well before that given in **CH**. Chester Herald says nothing about the early meetings between the Burgundians and Edward IV, but this is understandable in that his goal was only the record of the *emprise*. **AB** does give us more information on the other combats held after the main event, and it seems the French chroniclers were more interested in this than the English ones as the accounts of Olivier de La Marche (hereafter cited as **de La Marche**) and the anonymous continuator of the chronicle of Enguerrand de Monstrelet (hereafter cited as **Monstrelet**) make note of them as well.[33] That the dates are sometimes confused should not surprise us as the events took place over a significant period and, by chance, the itineraries could fit within a single year, rather than over two.

Where the accounts really cause problems for readers is in the details of the combats between Woodville and The Bastard. In particular it is the mounted combat on the first day that confuses things. All accounts that provide more than the barest record of the event, agree that something happened to The Bastard's horse, but what happened, and who was responsible, are in disagreement. **CH** mentions that during a meeting of

---

[32] *The Parliament Rolls of Medieval England 1275-1504 XIII: Edward IV 1461-1470*, ed. by R. Horrox, Parliament Rolls of Medieval England (Boydell, 2005), p. 250 (hereafter referred to as *PRME XIII*).

[33] The editions used here are Olivier de La Marche, *Mémoires d'Olivier de La Marche, maitre d'hotel et capitaine des gardes de Charles le Téméraire*, ed. by Henri Beaune and Jules d'Arbaumont (Librairie Renouard, Henri Loones, successeur, 1883) and Enguerrand de Monstrelet, *The Chronicles of Enguerrand de Monstrelet [...] Continued by Others to the Year 1516*, ed. by Bon-Joseph Dacier and Thomas Johnes (W. Smith, 1840).

the *emprise* organizers, held at St. Paul's, concerns were raised by The Bastard's party that they hoped to avoid a hazard encountered in a previous event involving one of the Bastard's men and a horse 'armed and enforced with three long daggers, one before and two on the sides.'[34] This foreshadowing for the *emprise* as the mounted combat ends prematurely when the Bastard's horse appears to injure itself on some part of the harness on Woodville's mount. The horse fell and, perhaps pinned The Bastard for a moment. **CH** describes a brief exchange where The Bastard is offered a second mount, but declines. **AB** describes the first clash, and exchange of blows, adding that The Bastard put a crack in Woodville's helmet and broke his own sword, but then his horse was injured (in the head and body) and fell, pinning The Bastard (who notably, maintained his defense on the way down). **AB** then notes that the horse bled profusely and died the following day (in the Herald's cordon, adjacent to the combat area). **De La Marche** specifies that The Bastard's horse was injured by the horn of Woodville's saddle and that it fell dead, instantly (although here, as before, The Bastard maintains his defense after the fall). According to this account, The Bastard accused Woodville of using the wrong equipment, making a remark to de La Marche afterwards that for the next stage of the *emprise* Woodville would have to face a man alone, and not a horse.

The accounts by Jehan de Wavrin and **Monstrelet** say nothing about the problems with horses but the entry in the English 'Gregory's chronicle' does acknowledge the injury and ultimate death of The Bastard's horse, saying he knows not how or by what means it happened. No mention of this incident appears in the account from the chronicle in the Cotton Vitellius or the Lambeth manuscripts and if the young Thomas Howard, Duke of Norfolk, was a witness to the first day, it made no impression on him.[35] This is implied by his vivid recollection of the axe combats of the second day.

The Great Chronicle of London entry on the *emprise* makes the claim that The Bastard's horse was blind, and that Woodville's horse had a spike or some other projection on a chamfron (or some other piece of harness over the head) and that this projection struck The Bastard's horse in the

---

[34] *Excerpta*, p. 200.

[35] The Cotton and Lambeth manuscript accounts are found in *Chronicles of London*, ed. by C. L. Kingsford (Clarendon Press, 1905), p. 92, 179. The edition of Howard's Chronicle, used here, is "Herne's Fragment" in J.A. Giles, ed., *The Chronicles of the White Rose*. (London: James Bohn, 1843), pp. 18–9.

mouth, causing it to rear-up and fall.³⁶ Woodville menaced the downed Bastard until the King intervened. This account does not claim the horse was killed, and even says that The Bastard was re-horsed, but no further combat took place. Robert Fabyan seems to combine **de La Marche**, who blamed the injury to the horse on Woodville's saddle horn and *The Great Chronicle of London* that blamed a metal spike on the Woodville's horse by blaming a metal spike on the saddle horn.³⁷ Accounts of the second day are less conflicted although some report more intense feeling than others and there is an impression that neither party was satisfied with the results.

AFTER THE *EMPRISE*

Anthony Woodville and The Bastard of Burgundy would encounter each-other again, proudly proclaiming themselves brothers-in-arms, in the summer of 1468, when next they competed in the *pas* honoring the wedding of Charles, Duke of Burgundy and Margaret of York, sister to Edward IV.³⁸ Woodville also retained the favor of the King but with it, his family continued to attract the envy and enmity of others. When the Earl of Warwick rose against Edward IV in 1469, Earl Rivers and his son Sir John Woodville were captured and executed following the July battle of Edgecote.³⁹ Anthony survived the brief return of Henry VI and participated in his downfall, serving Edward IV as Earl Rivers for the rest of his reign. However, Anthony stood in the way of Richard of Gloucester's ambitions to the throne and when the young Edward V was hustled into captivity, on 30 April 1483, so to was his guardian, Earl Rivers. He was executed at Pontefract on 25 June.⁴⁰

The Great Bastard of Burgundy served his half-brother Charles, now Duke of Burgundy, as diligently as he had served his father. When Charles died in combat in 1477, he would faithfully serve the Widowed Duchess Margaret. He was spared the fate of many contemporaries and died peacefully.⁴¹

---

³⁶ The edition used here is from *The Great Chronicle of London*, ed. by A. H. Thomas and I. D. Thornley (Printed by G.W. Jones at the sign of the Dolphin, 1938).

³⁷ The edition used here is Robert Fabyan, *The New Chronicles of England and France: In Two Parts*, ed. by H. Ellis (F. C. & J. Rivington; T. Payne; Wilkie and Robinson, 1811).

³⁸ A full account of this *pas*, translated and edited by Ralph Moffat, is in Baker-Grant and Damen, pp. 248–57.

³⁹ Michael Hicks, *Warwick the Kingmaker*, (Blackwell, 1998), p. 277.

⁴⁰ Charles Derek Ross, *Richard III* (Yale University Press, 1999), pp. 87–8.

⁴¹ Vaughan, *Charles the Bold*, pp. 235–39.

Editorial Conventions

In editing the English-language sources, modern usage for capitalization, punctuation, and word order are followed, where possible. Passages have been divided into sentences and paragraphs were doing so would improve readability. Unfamiliar terms or words borrowed from other languages, and which remain in the text, are explained in footnotes. The translations have tried to maintain the original structure and tone of the originals and any uncertainty about editorial choices are noted. Where possible, titles and places have been corrected to the modern usage, and where the correct spelling or identification is uncertain, they are left in *italics*. Unless otherwise stated, all translations are the work of the present author likewise, are all mistakes.

Bibliography

Manuscripts and Archival Sources

Utrecht University ms 1117 / hs 6b9

Printed Primary Sources

Bentley, S., ed., Excerpta Historica: Or Illustrations of English History (S. Bentley, 1831).
Calendar of the Patent Rolls Preserved in the Public Record Office: Edward IV, Henry VI, A.D. 1467-1477 (Public Records Office, 1900).
Enguerrand de Monstrelet, *The Chronicles of Enguerrand de Monstrelet [...] Continued by Others to the Year 1516*, ed. by Bon-Joseph Dacier and Thomas Johnes (W. Smith, 1840).
Fabyan, Robert, *The New Chronicles of England and France: In Two Parts*, ed. by H. Ellis (F. C. & J. Rivington; T. Payne; Wilkie and Robinson, 1811).
Horrox, R., ed., The Parliament Rolls of Medieval England 1275-1504 XIII: Edward IV 1461-1470, (Boydell, 2005).
Kingsford, C. L., ed., *Chronicles of London* (Clarendon Press, 1905).
La Marche, Olivier de, *Mémoires d'Olivier de La Marche, maitre d'hotel et capitaine des gardes de Charles le Téméraire*, ed. by Henri Beaune and Jules d'Arbaumont (Librairie Renouard, Henri Loones, successeur, 1883).
Schroeder, H. J., ed., Disciplinary Decrees of the General Councils (B. Herder, 1937).
Thomas, A. H., and I. D. Thornley, eds., *The Great Chronicle of London* (Printed by G. W. Jones at the sign of the Dolphin, 1938).

SECONDARY SOURCES

Barber, Richard, and Juliet R. V. Barker, *Tournaments* (Boydell Press, 1989).

Boulton, D'Arcy Jonathan Dacre, The Knights of the Crown: The Monarchical Orders of Knighthood in Later Medieval Europe: 1325-1520 (Boydell Press, 2000).

Brown-Grant, Rosalind, 'Art Imitating Life Imitating Art? Representations of the *Pas d'armes* in Burgundian Prose Romance: The Case of Jehan d'Avennes', in *The Medieval Tournament as Spectacle: Tourneys, Jousts and Pas d'Armes, 1100-1600*, ed. by Alan V. Murray and Karen Watts (Boydell & Brewer, 2020), p. 139–54.

Brown-Grant, Rosalind, and Mario Damen, eds., *Pas d'armes and Late Medieval Chivalry: A Casebook* (Liverpool University Press, 2025).

Bühler, Curt E, 'Sir John Paston's Grete Booke, a Fifteenth-Century "Best-Seller"', *Modern Language Notes*, 56, no. 5 (1941), p. 345–51.

Burton, Danielle, Anthony Woodville: Sophisticate or Schemer? (Amberley, 2024).

Damen, Mario, 'Tournament Culture in the Low Countries and England', in *Contact and Exchange in Later Medieval Europe Essays in Honour of Malcolm Vale*, ed. by Hannah Skoda (Boydell & Brewer, 2012), p. 247–66.

Hicks, M. A, *Warwick the Kingmaker* (Blackwell, 2002).

Hicks, M. A, 'Woodville [Wydeville], Richard, First Earl Rivers (d. 1469), Magnate', *Oxford Dictionary of National Biography*, online ed. (2011).

Higginbotham, Susan, The Woodvilles: The Wars of the Roses and England's Most Infamous Family (The History Press, 2013).

Jones, Robert W., Bloodied Banners: Martial Display on the Medieval Battlefield, Warfare in History (Boydell Press, 2010).

Kaeuper, Richard W., *Holy Warriors: The Religious Ideology of Chivalry* (University of Pennsylvania Press, 2009).

Kaeuper, Richard W., and Elspeth Kennedy, *The Book of Chivalry of Geoffroi de Charny: Text, Context, and Translation*. (University of Pennsylvania Press, 1996).

Khalaf, Omar, 'Patronage, Print and the Education of the Gentry in Late Medieval England: The Case of Earl Rivers's Dicts and Sayings of the Philosophers', in *Current Issues in Medieval England*, ed. by L. Vazzosi (Peter Lang, 2021), p. 46–58.

Lander, J. R., 'Marriage and Politics in the Fifteenth Century: The Nevilles and the Wydevilles', *Historical Research*, 36, no. 94 (1963), p. 119–52.

Levitt, Emma, 'Tiltyard Friendships and Bonds of Loyalty in the Reign of Edward IV, 1461-1483', in *Loyalty to the Monarchy in Late Medieval and Early Modern Britain, c.1400-1688*, ed. by Matthew Ward and Matthew Hefferan (Palgrave, 2020), p. 1–35.

MacCracken, H.N., 'The Flower of Souvenance: A Moment in the Twilight of Chivalry', *The Swanee Review*, 20, no. 3 (1912), p. 366–76.

Muhlberger, Steven, Deeds of Arms: Formal Combats in the Late Fourteenth Century (Chivalry Bookshelf, 2005).
Nadot, Sébastien, Rompez les lances! chevaliers et tournois au moyen âge (Autrement, 2010).
Pascual, Lucia Diaz, 'Jacquetta of Luxembourg, Duchess of Bedford and Lady Rivers (c. 1416-1472)', *The Ricardian*, 21 (2011), p. 67-91.
Pidgeon, Lynda, 'Antony Wydevile, Lord Scales and Earl Rivers: Family, Friends and Affinity Part 1', *The Richardian*, 15 (2005), p. 1-19.
Pidgeon, Lynda, 'Antony Wydevile, Lord Scales and Earl Rivers: Family, Friends and Affinity Part 2', *The Ricardian*, 16 (2006), p. 1-15.
Richmond, Colin, 'Woodville [Wydeville], Anthony, Second Earl Rivers (c. 1440-1483), Magnate', *Oxford Dictionary of National Biography*, online ed. (2011).
Ross, C. D., *Edward IV* (Yale, 1997).
Ross, C. D., *Richard III* (Yale University Press, 1999).
Vaughan, Richard, Charles the Bold: The Last Valois Duke of Burgundy, New ed (Boydell Press, 2002a).
Vaughan, Richard, Philip the Good: The Apogee of Burgundy, New ed (Boydell Press, 2002b).
Wagner, Anthony Richard, Heralds & Heraldry in the Middle Ages: An Inquiry into the Growth of the Armorial Function of Heralds, 2nd ed. (Oxford University Press, 1956).

CHAPTER 2

The Sources

Abstract There are 13 accounts of varying lengths, recording the events of the 1467 *emprise* between Anthony Woodville, Lord Scales and The Bastard of Burgundy. At least five of the accounts are confidently the work of eyewitnesses or active participants while the rest are either records at second-hand or composites of reported memory.

Keywords Chronicles • Chester Herald • Olivier de La Marche • Jehan de Wavrin • Enguerrand de Monstrelet • Robert Fabyan • *Pas d'armes* • Deeds of arms • Heralds • Court culture • Chivalry

CHESTER HERALD

[Adapted from *Excerpta Historica: Or Illustrations of English History*, ed. by S. Bentley (London: Samuel Bentley, 1831), pp. 176–212].

The longest English record of this *emprise* is from the perspective of the English Herald involved in organizing the event. Most surviving copies include copies of the correspondence (sometimes in their original French) between Woodville, The Bastard of Burgundy, and other officials involved planning the performance. There are at least four survivals of the narrative account (not all of which contain the extant correspondence) while some collections contain only the letters.[1] This sort of documented narrative was a popular English format for recording chivalric deeds of arms and several notable collections survive with associations with English knights and members of the upper gentry, including one of the participants on the English side, Sir John Astley.[2] Most readers were interested in the formal aspects of the correspondence and the language surrounding the ritual of the *emprise*, so it was not always aspiring members of the martial elite who took an interest.[3] **CH** is the only account of the *emprise* that contains the initial challenge given to Woodville by Queen Elizabeth's ladies-in-waiting, and the meeting between Woodville and Burgundy's representatives at St. Paul's Cathedral on 7 June. **AB** describes the presentation of the *emprise* in Woodville's letters and the arrival of Chester Herald with the *emprise*, but does not mention the meeting at St. Paul's'. This meeting was where the final details were established before the day of the event, and it is likely that Chester Herald was the only recorded of the *emprise* to also attend this meeting.

Chester Herald was one of Edward IV's officers attached to the royal household through the King's possession of the Palatinate of Chester. The individual who held the office in the 1460s was probably one John Water (or Walter) who served from 1455 until his dismissal in 1471.[4] As expected of a Herald whose primary function was the identification of elites and recording their actions, **CH** is full of historically identifiable characters and plenty more who remain obscure, but for their proximity to their chivalric employers. The lists in **CH** largely agree with those in **AB**, no doubt because the Burgundian source was also a herald. There are, however, errors accumulated from successive copyists and editors and by the time Samuel Bentley made this composite version, some names were difficult to decipher without a thorough familiarity with the characters from other sources. **CH** also has a habit of retaining some of the specialized French

---

[1] *Sir John Paston's 'Grete Boke': A Descriptive Catalogue, with an Introduction, of British Library MS Landsdowne 285*, ed. by G. A. Lester (D. S. Brewer, 1984), p. 103.

[2] Astley's collection includes an illustration of his own exploit of arms, and is now New York, Morgan Library MS M.775.

[3] G. A. Lester, 'The Literary Activity of the Medieval English Heralds', *English Studies*, 71, no. 3 (1990), pp. 222–29, and G. A. Lester, 'Fifteenth-Century English Heraldic Narrative', *The Yearbook of English Studies*, 22 (1992), pp. 201–12.

[4] Anthony Wagner, 'Chester Herald', in *College of Arms, Queen Victoria Street*, Survey of London Monograph 16, Walter H. Godfrey, ed. (London Survey Committee, 1963), pp. 119–129.

vocabulary used in relation to formal correspondence and staged combats which can be a challenge to modern readers but is itself important evidence for understanding what was likely considered common knowledge for Chester Herald's readers. **CH** was not written for a private audience or a small circle of Woodville's intimates. Rather it was a public work available to members of England's martial elite and gentry where it can be seen as a kind of aspirational text. This is certainly the case for the copy collected for Sir John Paston, who was an occasional tournament companion of Woodville but never participated in anything so dramatic or international in scale and scope as the *emprise* of the flower of remembrance.[5]

As one would expect from a Herald in royal service, **CH** presents a formal, diplomatically respectful, narrative that smooths over some of the obstacles that delayed the *emprise* and minimizes or omits some of the points of controversy that are more prominent in the other accounts. No mention is made of the two-year delay between the first letters from Woodville and the departure of the Bastard for London. There is a hint of the personal in praise **CH** has for his Burgundian hosts who sent Chester Herald back to England with generous gifts. special note is made of the great hospitality extended to Chester Herald at Burgundy's court. The description of the combats in **CH** are straightforward and carefully phrased to appear impartial but it does not overlook the incident with the Bastard's horse, even if the explanation is obscure. **AB** and **Monstrelet** are more critical, blaming Woodville with negligence or maliciousness. **CH** does not discuss the events following the combats of Woodville and The Bastard, and says nothing of the feasts and meetings with Edward IV, nor the death of the Duke of Burgundy, necessitating The Bastard's prompt return. Instead, **CH** ends with Edward IV's intervention in the foot combat.

Read on its own, **CH** feels entirely authentic, combining elements of the absurd (such as the injury to Burgundy's horse) with intense and earnest combat. One can understand how such staged violence could (and often did), escalate to a life-threatening stage. When read beside the other accounts, the accuracy, if not the verisimilitude, is challenged.

The edition reproduced here is adapted from that published first in 1831 by Samuel Bentley (and cited in the notes as *Excerpta*). Some of the spelling and structure has been modernized or corrected where there are obvious errors (either carried over from the original manuscript sources or

---

[5] See Bühler, 'Sir John Paston's Grete Booke, pp. 345–51.

introduced by later editors). Otherwise, the language and structure is preserved. Any significant changes to the copy text, or places where some clarification would aid reading, are given in the notes. Bentley placed some of the supplementary material (not always found with Chester Herald's account) in his footnotes but these have been extracted and placed in an appropriate chronological sequence within this edition.

Edited Transcription

The Acts of the full honourable and knightly arms done between the right noble Lords, Sir Anthony Woodville Lord Scales and of Newsells, brother to the most high and excellent Princess the Queen of England and of France and Lady of Ireland, challenger. And Sir Antoine the Bastard of Burgundy, Count of Roche and Lord of Beveren and Beuvry, defender, before the Earl of Worcester, then Great Constable of England, and [before] the most experienced and victorious Prince Edward IV, King of England and of France, Lord of Ireland, the 11th and 12th days of June in the 7th year of his reign at Smithfield.[6]

The fortune of the *emprise* of the said full noble and valorous knight, Sir Anthony Woodville:

The Wednesday next after the solemn and devout feast of the Resurrection of our blessed savior and redeemer, Jesus Christ, for some of my business at the departing from the high mass, I drew myself to the Queen of England and France and Lady of Ireland, my sovereign Lady, to which I am right humble subject. And as I spoke to her ladyship on knee, the bonnet [removed] from my head as ought. I know not by what adventure nor how it happened, until the ladies of her company arrived about me and they of their benevolence tied about my right thigh a collar of gold, garnished with jewelers-work and was made with one letter. And when I had it, it was nearer my heart than my knee. And to that collar was tied a noble flower of *Souvenance*, enameled, and in manner of an *emprise*. And then one of them said to me full demurely, that I should talk not of it worthy as at that time. And then they withdrew them all, each one in their places. And I, abashed of this adventure, rose myself up and went to thank

---

[6] English regnal years were counted from the date of the sovereign's accession which, for Edward IV was 4 March. Thus, the 7th regnal year began on 4 March 1467, and ending on 3 March 1468. See C. R. Cheney and Michael Jones, eds., *A Handbook of Dates for Students of British History*, new ed. (Cambridge: Cambridge University Press, 2000).

them all, of their right great honour that they did that time, and as I took up my bonnet that I had let fall nigh unto me, I found in it a bill written in small parchment rolled and closed with a little threat of gold, and sealed.

Then thought I, know that their-in was the countenance that by them was given me. Then I thanked right humbly the Queen, that of her good grace had suffered such honour to be done to me in so high a presence and also the ladies all of their honour [had] done to me.

That done, I went forth with the King, my sovereign Lord, to show unto his highness my adventure and the *emprise* that was [to] me charged. And humbly presented unto his highness the said bill so closed, meekly beseeching his good grace that it pleased him to give me that honour and grace to agree and consent to the will of the ladies in that party and that he would give me notice to accomplish the continuance in the said bill to be delivered. The King unclosed the said bill and commanded the same openly to be read in his high presence, in which was contained certain chapters, that so read the King of his abundant grace licensed me to accomplish the contents of the same:

THE prologue of the said Lord Scales after the reading of the said bill before the King and of the chapters contained in the same, for certain arms on horseback and on foot.

In the worshipful reverence and help of our blessed savior Jesus Christ, of the glorious Virgin his mother, and Saint George, [the] very tutor and patron and cry of Englishmen, in augmentation of knighthood and recommendation of nobility, also for the glorious school and study of arms and for the courage thereof to my power to maintain and follow, and for to avoid slothfulness of time lost, and to obey and please my fair lady, I, Anthony Woodville, Knight, Lord Scales and of Newsells, Englishman, [on the] 17th day of April, [the] year of our Lord **1465**, have received by the ladies the gift of a rich collar of gold and on that hanging a noble remembrance, the which, of their grace, have taken and set upon my right thigh. The which remembrance, by God's pleasure, notice, and license of the King my sovereign, I have taken the charge for [an] *emprise* to furnish and accomplish, with the help of God, the arms that follow.

The Chapters contained in the said bill for the arms on horseback

First. I shall be bound by express commandment to appear at the noble city of London at the day and hour that may shall be limited and ordered in the month of October next coming,[7] before the King, my said sovereign

---

[7] That is, October 1465.

Lord, or his commissioned deputy, my judge in that party, against a noble man of four [generations] lineages, and without any reproach, at my choice, if he will present him against me.

The Second Chapter

The second chapter is, that we shall assemble on horse, armed each at his pleasure, in saddles of war, without advantage of rests or improper devices.[8] And we shall run without any barrier with ground spear-heads, one course each, with spear only. And then we shall set the hands to the sharp swords and shall fight, be it with the point or with other strokes, to the advantage of every party, to the completion of 37 strokes are smitten between is two.

The Third Chapter

I shall do deliver spears and swords of the which my fellow shall have the choice.

The Fourth Chapter

And if it happened (that God defend) that one of us two is borne to the earth, out of his saddle, without a fall of the horse, and with stroke of spear or of sword, the arms then shall be held to be accomplished.

The Fifth Chapter

That if any of us two be hurt (that God defend) as from the spear and the sword, so that none has the power to finish, the arms shall be then held to be accomplished as abovesaid. This is touching the first arms.

The chapters of the second arms to be done upon foot

Item. I shall hold to present myself for the second time before the King my said sovereign Lord or his deputy, my judge in this party, at such a day as shall be to me assigned in the said month of October, against a noble man of conditions as is abovesaid, if that he present himself against me, to make furnish and accomplish the arms that follow.

The Second Chapter

That we shall be armed on foot, as two noble men in such a case appertains. And may bear targes and pavises to the pleasure of each of us. And we shall be weaponed of spears, axes, and daggers. And we shall cast each one of us only one spear, and then we shall fight with other weapons until the time that one of us be born to the earth or else by all points be put from the weapons.

---

[8] *Excerpta* uses the original French term *malingyne* which later is read as 'malignity' but here the more literal 'evil engines' more aptly applies, seemingly referring to similar mechanical aids like the previously rejected lance rests.

The Third Chapter
That I shall do deliver the said weapons of the which my fellow shall have the choice. And if any question or debate were had or moved of these present chapters to be evilly written or evilly understood, be it sure that the King shall ordain for this cause noble men that the differences shall be lightly appeased in the honour at the right of all parties.
The Conclusion
And for the final conclusion of these present chapters I shall be bound on my costs to be had and obtained of the King my sovereign Lord, a sure and sufficient safe-conduct to the noblemen that will do me the honour to come to me to fight according to the contents of my chapters. That they may come, abide, and return safely, and without any malignity, as well in the realm of England as in other Lordships appertaining to the King my said sovereign Lord, such time and time as that they will ask, and to such a number of men and horse as they will require, conveniently, and as in such a case appertaining.
The contents of a letter sent to the Lord Bastard from the Lord Scales by Chester Herald with the *emprise* after the said fortune and consent of the King, the said Lord to touch the same.
Right worshipful Lord, by these present chapters you see and know the charge in the which I am bound and held under the valor of a Lady, and that I am restrained by commandment and will, and I am named that I shall do these arms in this city of London and in this realm of England: The which thing I may not without disobeying enlarge or infringe, therefore to furnish and accomplish [that] which is commanded me and the contents of these present chapters, for the discharge of my heavy burden, to fulfill my long desire, and to appease my heart of the same, and for great and reasonable causes thereof moving me—as above—I have sent unto you in all affection and cordial request, Chester, Herald, and servant unto the King of England and of France, my sovereign Lord, to present you in my behalf these letters, these chapters, with the right noble Flower of Remembrance that hath been taken me and charged for an *emprise*, you beseech and requiring that it please you to show me so much honour and friendship for to touch the said flower, my *emprise*, and to accomplish the arms contained in these present chapters.

The which flower I sent over the sea unto you, as unto the most renowned knight, and unto the most readiest and determined in such noble works to accomplish. Without abasing any other, and that by counsel nor by enquiry made, I know no choice, nor know none such in any region. And for ever I bind me and mine in as much as God hath given me of good fortune to be yours, and long as the honour, the life, the goods may bear. And when the said Herald officer of arms, bearer of this *emprise* above said shall return to me, and have made his report, and held said flower worshiped and touched with so dignified and knightly hand as yours is, then shall the said flower [be] joyously by me taken again and shall make myself ready, and hear it as my most dearest thing, and the cause whereof I trust to draw much fruit of worship in this world, and unto the time that I have furnished and accomplished these present arms against you.

Right worshipful Lord, for as much as I consider that you, and to such, so high and so noble works may continually [fall] and much besides of coming, and many breakings to your high *emprise* as well, for the wars public often coming in your marches, accident of sickness, or the will of your sovereign, or the [ ]⁹ of your lady, that is not for the be disobeyed, of the which such points may suffice to such noblemen, as is reasonable and legitimate excuse to retard you and others of many high and honourable *emprises*.

This considered, to show unto you the worship, the desire, and affection that I bear unto you above all Knights, I have so much required and opportune that if it be thus that by one of these reasons of other true *essoine*,[10] you may not come abide and attend to the accomplishment of the said *emprise*, nor furnish the arms of the which I required [of] you, and support the burden of my charge, one whole year to take from the end of the said month of October unto the date of one whole year expired. That is to say, at all times during the said time of the year, I shall be held that you shall have me waiting late, for the arms to furnish according to the contents of my said chapters the which I promised you (but reasonable *essoine* overcome me, and worthy to my excuse) but I will accomplish the contents in the same. And that no man think that I do it or undertake the things abovesaid by any arrogance, presumption, envy, or any outrage to be called worthy, for upon God and my honour, I do it not but for to obey my fair lady and to have countenance of you and principally of a good Knight, the which you be my choice. So be it that the creator of heaven

---

⁹ *Excerpta* leaves a blank here.

[10] **CH** uses the Latin legal term for a valid excuse for failure to appear, used in English common law. See J. H. Baker, *An Introduction to English Legal History*, 4th ed. (Oxford University Press, 2007), p. 58.

and of earth, to the which I pray that he give you joy of your fair lady. Right worshipful Lord, and right noble and valorous and renowned Knight, to that intent that you be better ascertained that I will withhold, do and accomplish the things above said, I have sealed these present chapters with the seal of my arms, and signed with my hand, in the place and manor royal of Sheen, the 18th day of the month of April, the year 1465.

The Supplication of the said right noble Lord to the King, after the presentation of the said *emprise*, the King to command, and herald to receive, the *emprise* chapters aforesaid, and to deliver the same to the right noble Lord the Bastard of Burgundy. The King's commandment to Chester Herald thereupon.

The manner of receiving thereof by the Herald. And the King's commandment to his Constable of England.

The said *emprise* with the said chapters as is abovesaid, presented to the King's highness, being in his high chamber of estate in his manor of Sheen, accompanied with many noble Lords, the said right noble and worshipful Lord Sir Anthony Lord Scales and Newsells etc., full well advisedly and due obeisance before the King's good grace in Godley words beseeched his highness on the most humble wise to license one of his Heralds named Chester, to receive the said *emprise* which he proposed to send unto the right worshipful Knight, the Bastard of Burgundy, with the said chapters for arms on horseback and on foot to be profited. To which the King well agreed. Then the said Chester [Herald] in the coat-armor of the said noble and worshipful Lord [Scales] was commanded by the same according to his office of arms to obey and assess his desire granted upon so high and worshipful a courage. The which done the said Chester received the same *emprise* named the Flower of Remembrance and it set upon a kerchief of pleasance, took the charge of the delivering thereof and so departed. And immediately then the King's highness commanded the Earl of Worcester, great Constable of England, there being present, to enact and remember that memorable act and entry of the worshipful arms with the mercy of our Lord, to the accomplishment in his royal presence, between him and the said noble Knight, the Bastard of Burgundy, according to the which commandment the Constable said his high commandment should be performed according to the duty of his office.[11]

---

[11] John Tiptoft, 1st Earl Worcester (1427–1470) a knight of the Garter, he was highly educated and well-traveled, rising to high offices that included steward of Edward IVs household and constable of the Tower of London. He also earned Earl Warwick's enmity and there

The Presentation of the Lord Scales letter aforesaid and the said *emprise* by Chester Herald to the Lord Bastard at Brussels the last day of April, the year abovesaid, reverently done in full high presence. And the touching of the same by the said Lord Bastard, licensed so to do by the Duke of Burgundy, with reverent obedience to the said *emprise*.

The which last day of April the said Chester entered the town of Brussels and sent a Pursuivant from his lodging unto the Lord Bastard of Burgundy, showing him that he was come out of England with a letter from the said Lord Scales. My said Lord Bastard of Burgundy sent two Heralds and two Pursuivants and conveyed him before the Duke's lodging where he was accompanied with diverse estates. The said Herald Chester presented his letter and charges to him as answered. Right high and noble Count, my right honourable Lord Anthony Woodville, Lord Scales and Newsells, brother of the excellent and right high and mighty Princess, Queen of England and of France, with all due reverence recommend him to you and send you this letter. I meekly beseech you that it may please your lordship to see this writing and read it or do to make it to be read, that I may have such an answer as my said right honourable Lord may be satisfied and my power honestly said. Then answering the said noble Lord to the said Herald, it shall be seen and read and indeed in haste in such way answered as of right you shall hold you content. And soon after the said answer, the said Lord Bastard departed with all the company of Lords and went before the presence of the Lord Charles and showed him a letter and articles in such wise as all the Lords went unto the Duke's presence for the direction, the last day of April rehearsed aforesaid. And on the morning the first day of May, there was commanded that all the heralds and Pursuivants in the court of Burgundy should come to Chester's lodging and so bring him to the presence of the Duke on horseback, The said Chester proceeding into the presence, in this way as follows.

Right high and mighty Prince. Right humbly I beseech you of your highness to license me to show in your presence my charges and errands the which I have received in the high presence of the King of England and of France my sovereign Lord, by my right honourable Lord Anthony Woodville, Lord Scales and Newsells, brother unto [the] excellent and right high and mighty princess Queen of England and of France, my

---

was little public grief over his execution following Henry VI's brief return to the throne in 1470: B. Kohl, "Tiptoft, John, 1st Earl of Worcester," in *Oxford Dictionary of National Biography*, online ed. (2004).

sovereign Lady, touching the noble Lord Bastard of Burgundy, Earl of Roche, and Lorde of Beveren and Beuvry.

The Duke answering the said Herald in this form: 'Do your charge, we license you.' Then the said Heralds of the court and Pursuivants went into another chamber beside the Duke's chamber and took the Lord Scales' coat of arms upon his [Chester Herald's] body and the *emprise* born high, between his hands in a kerchief of [pleasance] honorably, the *emprise* being fastened onto the uppermost border of the said kerchief, and covered with the lowest border of the kerchief and thus bringing it honorably, making three obeisance in the approaching of the presence, and after the third obeisance letting fall the lower border of the kerchief which covered the *emprise*, and stood up upon the right hand of the prince there being in state. And then the Duke gave in commandment to a Lord, a brother of the *Toison* to read to them on high my Lord Scales' letter and articles.[12] And all that time the Herald, holding the *emprise* on high in the said presence of the Duke, and asked license to touch the *emprise* and to accomplish the articles there read, signed and sealed with the seal of arms of the said Lord Scales. And then the said Lord Bastard came unto the *emprise*, saying to the Chester Herald:

I pray you recommend right humbly to my Lord Scales, my brother, as heartily as I can. I thank him right highly of the honour that he does to me by his writing, to the edifying, and increasing of honour. And to the fulfilling of his honourable request, I take upon me by license of my Prince to touch this *emprise* and obliged me to accomplish these, his articles.

And with that touching, making a reverent obedience. And then Burgundy took the furthest edge of the kerchief of pleasance in the which the *emprise* was born, and Charles the other part [of the kerchief], and so covered the said *emprise* worthily, as it came unto the presence before rehearsed.

And then the said Chester [Herald] kneeling before the Duke, saying as follows. 'Right high and my prudent Prince, meekly I beseech you to pardon me of my simpleness and of my rude speaking.'[13] The Duke answering 'Chester, you are right welcome!' There Chester bearing the

---

[12] A 'brother of the *Toison*' indicates a member of the Order of the Golden Fleece. This Order was founded in 1431 by Phillip the Good on the occasion of his marriage to Isabella of Portugal (D'Arcy Jonathan Dacre Boulton, *The Knights of the Crown: The Monarchical Orders of Knighthood in Later Medieval Europe; 1325–1520* (Boydell, 2000), pp. 356–98).

[13] Here **CH** is likely making a formal, and probably traditional, apology for the quality of his French when addressing the Duke of Burgundy directly.

emprise so touched in the presence and the sight of all people, and there placed it in a chamber apart as appertained. And on the morning next coming, the said Lord Bastard desired Chester to have patience. He durst not move might deliver him an answer, without consultation of the Duke. And so, the said Chester abode there daily with a great cheer, as pertained a Herald to have, accompanied with ancient Kings of Arms and noble Heralds, nine days following.

And the tenth day he was delivered with a letter to the Lord Scales with all due recommendation. And as brotherly he desired my Lord Scales to take him in anything that is possible and honorably him to do, as well before his accomplishing of his act, as after the said act. The said Lord Bastard sent to Burgundy his Herald, a rich gown furred with sable, the which he wore at the touching of [the] noble *emprise* before rehearsed, and his doublet of black velvet garnished with arming pointes, and the styles of the doublet sleeves clasped with clasps of gold, and 40 Renes Gilders, to the said Chester [Herald].

According to the commandment and ordinance [Chester Herald] received the said gifts and then dressed himself in the same, and came into the court and reverently thanked and took his leave and departed. And then the said Heralds of the court accompanied the said Chester [Herald] a league out of the town of Brussels.

Here follows the names being present at the touching of the *emprise*:
The right high and mighty Prince, the Duke of Burgundy
The Count Charles[14]
Lord Jehan of Bourbon
Lord Adolf of Cleves[15]
The Prince of 'Dorenge'[16]
Lord Jehan of Luxemburg[17]
Lord Roussy[18]
Lord of Arguel[19]

---

[14] Charles, Count of Charlois, eldest son of Philip the Good.
[15] Lord of Ravenstein.
[16] Spelled 'Dorenge' in *Excerpta*. There are many candidates for this particular prince of Orange, but it is likely one related to the two men that follow in the list.
[17] This may be Jacques du Luxembourg, bastard of Saint-Pol.
[18] Likely Antoine de Luxembourg, Lord of Roussy.
[19] 'Dargue' in *Excerpta*. This is likely Jean IV de Chalon, Lord of Arguel and son of the Prince of Orange.

The Marshal of Burgundy[20]
Lord Montaigne[21]
Lord Moreuil[22]
Lord of *Vittiaux*
Lord of Roche[23]
Sir Simon de Lalaing[24]
Lord Miraumont[25]
Lord Crèvecoeur[26]
Sir Philip of Bourbon[27]
Lord Countay
Lord Monsures[28]
Sir Antoine *de P'teney*[29]
Lord Tienges
Sir Antoine de Lalaing
Sir Martin de *Trapezonde*[30]
John de Chassa[31]
Ernalt Bouton[32]
Dreux de Humières[33]

---

[20] At the time this was Thibaud IX de Neuchâtel (Vaughan, *Philip the Good*, p. 389).
[21] Perhaps Jacques de Fouilleuse, Lord of Concy and Montagny.
[22] Waleran de Soissons, Lord of Monreuil died around 1464 so this may be his heir (Brown-Grand and Damen, p. 213, n.).
[23] Philippe Pot, Lord of La Roche-Nolay abd Châteauneuf (c.1428–93) and councillor-chamberlain of Philip the Good (ibid., p. 213, n.).
[24] Simon de Lalaing (c.1405–77), Lord of Montigny and chamberlain of Philip the Good (ibid., p. 232 n.).
[25] (Miralmont in *Excerpta*) Robert, Lord of Miraumont.
[26] (Crieucure in *Excerpta*) Philippe de Crèvecoeur (Brown-Grant and Damen, p. 334).
[27] Likely the Philippe of Bourbon, chamberlain to Charles the Bold in 1474. He was probably knighted between 1463-5 (Brown-Grant and Damen, p. 420 n.).
[28] An otherwise unspecified member of the major Picardy family and perhaps the Lord of Monsures listed among the participants in the *pas d'armes de Sandricourt* of 1493 (ibid., p. 266 n.).
[29] Perhaps Antoine de Pountevès, Lord of Cabanes (ibid., p. 132).
[30] This sounds like the Trebizond of Anatolian Byzantium but this may be coincidence.
[31] Also known as Jean de Beneton, he was Lord of Mounet by 1468 when he participated in the *Pas de Arbe d'or* (ibid., p. 491).
[32] Most likely this is Phillipe Bouton, who appears in **AB.**
[33] 'Drues of Hunieres' (*Excerpta*) was a courtier of Philip the Good from at least 1463 (Brown-Grant and Damen, p. 420 n.).

John de Massy[34]
Charles, Marshall of arms of Brabant
Fuselles Pursuivant of arms[35]
N'ul ne sy fret, Pursuivant of arms[36]

The return of Chester Herald with the *emprise* touched by the Lord Bastard, and his relation to the King at Greenwich.

Then present, the Duke of Gloucester, the Duke of Buckingham, the Earl of Worcester, Constable of England, and the Earl of Shrewsbury, the 23rd day of May, the year abovesaid.[37]

Right high and excellent Prince, most Imperial King. I have been according to the high charges the which I received in your excellent presence in your manor royal of Sheen, the Wednesday after the feast of Easter, by my Lord Scales, and by the license of the right high and mighty Prince, the Duke of Burgundy, there presented my Lord's *emprise* under this forum as I have it here in your presence. Meekly I beseech you of your abundant grace to be pleased with my rude behavior and the require of honour high presence received this his *emprise*, touched by the high and noble Lord Antoine Bastard of Burgundy, Count of La Roche, Beveren, and Beuvry, he obliging him to me your Herald, to accomplish the articles and his noble valor and have given me charge to recommend him as brotherly as he can. And then proceeding, show the *emprise* by the King's commandment unto the Lord Scales leg, reverently, and there foisted it onto a collar of gold upon the same.

And then the said Chester [Herald] approached again into the high presence of the King, saying these words: Excellent King and my most good and gracious sovereign Lord, meekly I beseech you of your abundant grace, that it may please you to thank my Lord Scales of the honour that he put me to occupy in so high a matter. And also I beseech you to owe thanks unto my Lord Bastard, the which gave me this same rich gown

---

[34] (Massey in ***Excerpta***) Was a cupbearer of Philip the Good (Ibid., p. 195 n.).

[35] Heraldic term for a firesteel, one of the emblems associated with the Order of the Golden Fleece (Boulton, *Knights of the Crown*, p. 366).

[36] Later this is rendered as *null ne cy frete*, in **AB**, which is read as 'none shall touch me.' Presumably this was a motto associated with a particular lord or title and was used to refer to the corresponding Pursuivant, in the same way that others are named for badges.

[37] These are Richard, the King's youngest brother (who was between 16 and 17) Henry Stafford (Duke of Buckingham), the King's ward (who would have been about nine). The Earl of Shrewsbury was John Talbot.

and this doublet garnished in this form, the which he wore at the touching of the *emprise* and 40 florins and my costs the time of my being there.

The copy of the certification made by the Earl of Worchester, High Constable of England.

To all Princes, Dukes, Earls, Barons, Knights, and other noblemen, learned and expert in noble deeds of arms, John, Earl of Worcester, Lord Tiptoft, and of Powys, High Constable of England, greeting and increase of all worthiness. Where, by the virtue of the said office to us commanded, it appertained not only to do, put in writing, all the noble notable deeds of arms which in our time have been accomplished to the intent that they should remain and abide in remembrance but also to the intent that the things right worthily begun should openly be notified in fair realms and regions and that other worthy men to their example should incline them to apply to such and similar deeds. And that by such noble exercises of arms the augmentation of worthy Knighthood should be the more and longer continued.

We let you know by these presents that the 19th day of the month of April, the year of our Lord 1465, in the chamber of estate in the Royal manor of Sheen, unto the excellence of the right high, right mighty, and right Christian Prince Edward, by the grace of God, King of England, my sovereign Lord, a right worthy Knight, Sir Anthony Woodville, Lord of Scales and Newsells, brother unto the right high and mighty Princess, the Queen my sovereign Lady, him presented, bearing a flower of remembrance for *emprise* of arms on horseback and on foot which was charged him to do and accomplish. The which kneeling right meekly besought the majesties Royal of the King, my said sovereign Lord, that it might please him of his grace to command unto Chester the Herald then being present, to receive the said flower of remembrance and the same to bear beyond the sea for to present and deliver for, and in the name of the said Lord Scales, to the noble and renowned Knight the Bastard of Burgundy. The which thing the King granted right benignly and commanded to the Herald so to do. Which received the flower, clothed and revested with the coat of arms containing the manner of the *emprise* of the said flower. The which Herald goes now beyond the seas for the same cause.

These things above said so done in our presence, the King, my said sovereign Lord hath commanded us to witness by our letters testimonial under the seal of the office that we use to seal with. Which thing we have done and do by these presents, given at London under the seal of our office of Constable, the 22nd day of the month of April the year of our

Lord 1465 and the 5th year of the reign of the King, my said sovereign Lord, Edward the 4th of this name since the Conquest of England.

Here follows the copy of the letter sent by the Bastard of Burgundy, answering the said articles and writings.

Noble and worshipful Lord, I recommend me to your remembrance as heartily and as certainly as is to me possible and thank you as affectionately and by the most express devotion that I can or may do, of your right joyful and desired tidings that by Chester the Herald you have written and sent unto me, with the right honourable and to me agreeable present that by the same you have done to offer and present by solemn honour and magnificence. That is to say, your noble *emprise* together with the high and Knightly articles directed unto me by right honourable mean: Whereof soon after so much and so much I thank you that I in no wise could well recite. For by the same with your gentle letters you do unto me so great worship and lovingness and friendship not deserved that I all my life for nothing could recompense nor deserve. Now it is so, noble and worshipful Lord, that for the great goodness and virtues renowned and published of you and of your Knighthood, and as you recite by your writings, I have heretofore desired and intended to have proffer and alliance with you for to discharge you of your burden to accomplish your *emprise* to please and agree to your honourable request. I have this day, the first day of May, touched the rich remembrance, your *emprise* and have accepted the contents of the articles to me from you presented, to the intent with God's help to pass into the realm of England at the time and day which in the said articles is ordained, for to accomplish our arms. And but if it be by the countenance of the war where I am now occupied, or by other so lawful letting, that the excuse by worship and reason generally I might not pass nor attend to the furnishing of this *emprise* at the first journey that by your articles you name and order, at this next day of October, be you sure that I shall dispose me by all the devotion and means to me possible to come at the second term that your nobleness hath granted me and shall warn you and do you to know two months before, like as you desire me. Requiring you that of your party in likewise you will so dispose and order your doings that you desire of us both may come to every effect. And for this time, I write none other thing to you but I pray to the Redeemer of mankind, Jesus Christ, to give your ample desires. Written at Brussels and signed with my own hand, the 4th day of May. Your beholden Burgundy. To the noble and worshipful Lord and my desired brother the Lord Scales and of Newsells.

Letter dispatched by the said Lord Scales to the said Lord, the Bastard of Burgundy.[38]

Most honored and most noble Sir, I recommend myself to you, and would have you know by this Herald, I see and understand, your gracious and most comforting letters together with the very pleasant news written at Brussels on the fourth of May, by which Herald your letters, signed by your hand, that on the first of the month of May, you touched the noble flower of remembrance—my *emprise*—that I sent to you by my Herald. The which you having so touched, I have joyfully received from which honour that has been done so cordially and affectionately that in this world I would not be able to thank you, and also of the good cheer and generosity shown to my Herald. The which keeps me, and will keep me, all this time in obligation [to you]. And that, notwithstanding, the impediment of war or impeded by other worthy *essoins* and reasonable excuses, that you will come to pass, in this Kingdom, to relive me of my vow whose relief I most humbly thank you.

The coming of the Bastard to Gravesend the 29th day of May, worshipfully accompanied, where Garter [Herald] met him at the King's commandment.

The Friday 29th day of May, the year of our Lord 1467 at the 7th year of the victorious, renowned Prince, King Edward the 4th, the Bastard of Burgundy accompanied with many noble Lords, knights, squires, and others about the number of 400. With four fore-castled caravels, richly appareled and enforced with all the manner habiliments of war, pennons, banners, guidons, streamers, his coat [of arms] also hanging with *arras* within and without, richly seen, came before Gravesend about the hour of four in the afternoon.[39] Whereas was ordained by the King's commandment, Garter King of Arms, and had lay there the space of three weeks before, to meet with him at his landing, where it ever had been, and to

---

[38] The letter following is translated from the French version found in *Excerpta*, pp. 194–6. This was extracted from the latter additions to the Paston *Grete Boke*. The letter also appears in London, British Library, MS Harley 4632 f. 88r. The second letter, also from Lord Scales, and dated the 13th of November is substantially the same as the first letter, but thanks to the several layers of transcription by non-French reading scribes, the version in *Excerpta* steadfastly resists easy translation and so it is omitted here, for the sake of the reader.

[39] *Arras* was a richly decorated fabric, often found in wall hangings and other furnishings rather than garments, and named for the location that was associated with its manufacture (Rebecca Olson, *Arras Hanging: The Textile That Determined Early Modern Literature and Drama* (University of Delaware Press, 2013)).

have conveyed him forth, and also to certify the King's highness of the same. The which as soon as he came in sight, the said Garter took and dressed a barge cleanly seen, met with him 2 miles off before he came there, and welcomed him hither. And desired him if he had liked to come to London and to rest him after his great labor. He answered that he was not disposed to land in any wise or [spend] time there, before he should perform his act. But there he would abide that night, and cast anchor before the town.

The meeting of the Bastard at the Blackwall by the Constable, worshipfully accompanied etc. The 30th day of May.

On the morning after Saturday, 30th day of May, he set up sail toward London and [in] the space of a mile he came to Greenwich, at the Blackwall, came to receive and to meet with him the Earl of Worcester, Constable of England, accompanied with many other Lords, Knights, Squires, and many Aldermen and rich commoners of the City of London, ordered in seven barges and all gaily arrayed to the number of [ ] And there welcomed him [Burgundy] and conveyed him forth to London.[40] And when he had cast anchor a little beneath Saint Katherine's,[41] received him and his fellowship of nobles and others into their [the Alderman's] barges and landed at Billingsgate,[42] whereas were also to welcome him many other Lords, nobles, Knights, Squires, and noble commoners of the said City. And from thence [he] was conveyed on horseback by the said Constable and Lords through Cornhill and Cheap, and by Saint Paul's of London, into the Bishop of Salisbury's palace at Fleet-street, the which was ordered by the King and richly appareled with arras and hanged with beds of cloth-of-gold, for his lodging within the town with all manner other stuff in and without the town for his disport. And to inspect his harness secretly, was ordered the Bishop's place at Chelsea, two miles, the one from the other. He to take his barge or his boat at such time as it liked him to do, for his pleasure.

The coming of the King to London after the coming of the Bastard, and the solemn meeting of them.

---

[40] Blank in *Excerpta*.

[41] St. Katharine's Hospital, on the North shore of the Thames, East of the Tower of London.

[42] Location of a landing on the North shore, between London Bridge to the West and the Tower of London to the East.

The Thursday next after, that is the 2nd day of June, came riding from Kingston upon Thames, through London, the King, which was met two miles before he came to town, with many Princes, Dukes, Earls, Barons, Knights, Esquires, the Mayor, Alderman, Sheriffs, and commoners of the city to the number of [ ].[43] Kings of arms, also Heralds and Pursuivants, in coats of arms as well as divers other Lords as of the same. As it belonged to the Prince Royal, with the sound of clarions, trumpets, *shalmose*, and others.[44] The King so royally conveyed, by the Constable bearing his baton in his right hand, the Earl Marshall, likewise in his left hand, the Lord Scales bearing the King's sword in the midst between both as well was met with [a] procession of the four orders without the town, as with other religious persons, priests, and clerks etc., as at Saint Paul's with procession solemn of Bishops, many mitered, with incense, received him into the Church with procession to the high alter, where he offered [thanks]. And then [the King] took his horse and rode through Fleet-street where the Bastard and his fellowship beheld the King coming. At the more was supposed because the Lord Scales bore the sword before the King.[45] And the Lord Scales, perceiving that, turned his horse suddenly and beheld him [Burgundy] the which was the first sight and knowledge personally between them. And so, from thence to Westminster where the King held and began his Parliament on the morning after.[46]

The presentation of the Bastard to the King after his coming.

The same day the Bastard there presented himself before the King with due reverence, desiring his day of battle to be prefixed. The which in likewise was desired on behalf of the Lord Scales, by the Earl Rivers his father, as hastily as it might please the King's highness. The King calling his council to him, commanded the Sheriffs of London to make the barriers to be made in Smithfield, the which by the advice of the Constable called to him the King's arms, the said barriers were made in length, containing four score and ten yards, and in breadth, four score yards of a size. And the field made firm, and stable assigned. The day to keep between them the Monday next ensuing. On Thursday, Saint Barnabee's day, the eleventh day of the

---

[43] Blank in the original.

[44] Possibly a phonetic rendering of 'shawm', a type of woodwind instrument (Anthony Baines, *Woodwind Instruments and Their History*, 3rd ed. (New York: Dover, 1977/1991), pp. 230–5).

[45] The intended meaning of this sentence is unclear.

[46] Edward IV issued writs of summons for this Parliament on 28 February with the opening date as 3 June: Horrox, *PRME XIII*, p. 250.

month of June. And prorogued his said Parliament therefore from the Wednesday before, unto the Monday next after.

The coming of the Lord Scales to London, nobbily accompanied to do his arms with the Bastard.

And on the Friday came the said Lord Scales in a barge richly seen, from Greenwich, four miles out of London, where he had tarried long and many a day, abiding the coming of the said Bastard, with many nobles in his company, arrived at St. Katherine's beside the Tower of London, where he was received by the Constable and Marshall and the Treasurer of England,[47] with many other noble Lords, Knights, Squires, in great number, [who] conveyed him through London, on horseback, in a long gown of rich cloth-of-gold tissue, a Herald and a Pursuivant bearing his coats of arms before him unto the Bishop's place of Ely in Holborn.[48] Where he kept solemn and worshipful household, richly seen, with rich *arras* of silk and clothes of gold.

The chapters held at Paul's by the said Constable for declaration of doubts moved by him upon the chapters.

The said Constable, as well the council of the Lord Scales and of the Lord Bastard's [council] being present, moved and enquired, first the council of the said Lord Scales, if there were any doubt that they could find in the chapters of the Lord Scales, to him [Burgundy] sent? The council of the said Bastard said that the chapters were right good and honourable so that there may [be] no great difficulty found in them. And showed a like act of pleasance done lately before their sovereign Lord the Duke of Burgundy, between a Knight of his and a squire of Germany, the which came to do his arms on horseback, the horse armed and enforced with thee long daggers, one before and two on the sides. The said Duke, seeing this, called his counsel, though of reason for as much as it was but an act of *pleasance* to the augmentation of the province of Knighthood, the which ought to be done with men's hands, ordered the said harness to be avoided.[49] And if any such like case fell, they report them to the King's highness and his council.

---

[47] These were the Earl of Worcester (Constable) John Mowbray, Duke of Norfolk (Marshal) Earl Rivers (Treasurer).

[48] Meaning, the Bishop of Ely's palace in Holborn.

[49] This refers to the distinction between a *pas d'armes* fought *á plaisance* (for pleasure) rather than *á outrance* (to the extreme), meaning that since the combat was not antagonistic, that such dangerous equipment was not appropriate (Will McLean, 'Outrance and Plaisance', *Journal of Medieval Military History*, VIII (2010), pp. 155–70).

Also, the Bastard's council demanded a question upon the second chapter of the arms on foot. Whereas it is said in the said chapter 'And we shall fight with spear, axe, and daggers, and we shall cast each of us only a spear, and then we shall fight with other weapons until the time that one of us is born to the ground' whether the intent was that the hand, the knee, or the whole body should be brought to the ground or one of them? It was considered by council thereof, the Lord Scales, that the one or the other should be brought to ground.

Also, where it was doubted in the said second chapter upon the casting of the spear it was agreed before the Constable by the council of both parties that each of them should cast his spear only, according to the said second chapter, without making of any other defense with the same.[50]

Also afterwards it was moved by the Constable, because of certain ambiguities to his seeming, concerning the said chapters to both council upon the second chapter on horseback. Where it is said 'We shall assemble on horse armed, each at his pleasure, in saddle of war without a rest, or malign help, and we shall run without any barrier, with ground spear heads, one course each, with spear only. and then we shall set the hands to the sharp swords and shall fight, be it with the thrust or other strokes, to the advantage of every party, to the accomplishment of 37 strokes be smitten between us two'. That if the case fell that any of the horse were stricken by any of the parties that the horse might not endure, the performing of the said arms should be accomplished, or no?

This was answered by both council that neither the Lord Scales nor Bastard intended not to hurt any others hose, and if the case fell so, that it should to change and make another [horse] to accomplish the arms.

Also in likewise, at the pleasure of the King, if any of their swords fall from them, in running of the said courses, by misfortune, before the strike with them, the said swords to be restored.

Also it was concluded by both council, that each should have a man to help them to change their spears, if they liked.

Also upon the third chapter, where it is said 'I shall do deliver spears and swords of the which my fellow shall have the choice. It was concluded by both council that after the spears be delivered each to purvey his want plate at his pleasure.

---

[50] In other words, the spears were only for throwing and could not be used for any other purpose, and no other actions could progress in the combat until the spears were thrown.

Also moved by the Constable of the 5th chapter: 'And if it happened (that God defend) that one of us two be born to the earth out of the saddle, without [the] fall of the horse, and with stroke of the spear or of the sword, the arms then shall be held to be accomplished.' It was answered by the Bastard's council that it should be at the King's will.

Also moved by the council of the Bastard, if any of them would charge with a hose the which was terrible to smite or bite[51] through which the one party might prevail against the other, and take advantage by the horse, which the said Bastard's council said that he never intended.

Answered by the Lord Scale's council that he never intended nor purposed to advantage himself by the means of a horse, but by his hands and due means of knighthood. And if he had any such horse he intended not, nor would, [ride] on his back, but utterly refuse him.

Also it was moved by the council [of the Bastard] if the case fell that any of them by way of feat, be put from his sword, whether it be lawful for him to lay hand on his fellow by the neck or engage him in any other wise?

This was remitted in as much as March, King of Arms, went unto Lord Scales and showed the said remission. The Lord Scales sent the aforesaid King of Arms to the Constable of England and charged him to say that he would not be agreeable to the said remission, but that each might engage himself with hand and sword at his desire. And then the Constable charged the said King of Arms to show it to the Lord Bastard.[52]

The Lord Scale's council:
The Earl of Douglas[53]
Sir John Astley[54]
Sir Lawrence Rayneford

---

[51] Meaning a horse notorious for biting or striking out.

[52] Meaning that this question was not resolved at the meeting described, but instead brought to Scales afterwards, through the office of March King of Arms. Scales seems to answer that he would not engage further, if he lost his sword, but did not want to keep The Bastard from choosing to act differently, if placed in the same position.

[53] James Douglas, 9th Earl Douglas (d. 1488).

[54] Also spelled 'Ashley', he was an experienced tourneyer under Henry VI (Kingsford, *Chronicles of London*, p. 150), a fixture of the Tower of London (Harris Nicolas, ed., *Proceedings and Ordinances of the Privy Council of England* ... (Printed by G. Eyre and A. Spottiswoode, 1837), vol. VI, p. 59) and briefly commander of the castle of Alnwick and prisoner of Lancastrian dissidents (Cora L. Scofield, *The Life and Reign of Edward the Fourth, King of England and of France and Lord of Ireland* (London: Longmans, Green, 1923), vol. I, p. 287).

The Lord Bastard's council:
Sir Simon de Lalaing[55]
Mr. Claude de Toulongeon[56]
Mr. Peter *de Wassue*[57]
Mr Philip *de Cohane*
M Phillip, Bastard of Brabant[58]
M Monferont[59]
M. Forestres, Officer of the Order of the Golden Fleece

The King's commandment to the Constable to purvey a convenient place for the field.
Thereupon the King our sovereign Lord commanded his Constable of his realm of England to go to his city of London and to take with him the King of Arms and Heralds to purvey a convenient place for the Arms. And then the Constable commanded the Mayor and the Mayor commanded the Sheriffs of London to make the lists. Which Sheriffs, by the commandment of the Constable, called to them the King's Heralds of the office of Arms, ordained the field to be made in length 4 score and ten, and in breadth, 4 score.[60] The field environed with [posts] 7 1/2 foot above ground, and 3 foot in the ground, pitched between every post, 3 mortises. In every mortis, from post-to-post, bars, 3 1/2 inch thick, 5 inch in breadth.[61] The field sufficiently sanded as appropriate. The King's place of judgement, 6 paces nearer the West end than the East end.
The coming of the Lord Scales to Saint Bartholomew,[62]

---

[55] *de La Laing* in **Excerpta**. This is the Lord of Montigny.
[56] *G. Launde* in **Excerpta**. This is Claude de Toulongeon, Lord of La Bastie, lieutenant of the Marshal of Burgundy (Baker-Grant and Damen, p. 256 n.).
[57] Possible *van Wassenaar*.
[58] Lord of Kruibeke and La Fertè, and was a chamberlain of Philip the Good (Baker-Grand and Damen, p. 197 n.).
[59] Probably Jean de Montfort, who participated in the *Pas du Chevalier au Cygne*, 1454 (Ibid., 406 n.).
[60] This converts to roughly 90 × 80 yards.
[61] Late-Tudor historian of London, John Stow, describes the field using a different standard of measure but makes the point clear that there were two concentric barriers with a 'five-foot' space between the inner and outer circuit (John Stow, *A Survey of London: Reprinted from the Text of 1603, with Introduction and Notes*, ed. by C.L. Kingsford (Clarendon Press, 1908), vol. II, pp. 32–3).
[62] Referring to the grounds of St. Bartholomew's Priory, which faced onto Smithfield from the East.

joining the East part of the field to do his arms.

The 10th day of June at afternoon, he took his horse and with great triumph and royalty was conveyed with many noble Dukes, Earls, Barons, Knights, Squires, etc. with minstrels, into St. Bartholomew's, joining the East part of Smithfield, where the barriers were made, and lodging there that night to put him in his devotion of his *emprise*.

The orders and keeping of the field

The Thursday the 11th day of June, the King commanded his Constable and Marshall to order and provide for the keeping of the said field, to be kept with sergeants of arms, armed. The barriers with their men. The emptying of the field with the Constable and Marshall. And after the Constable and Marshall ordered the said field to be set at every other post, a man of arms, and at every corner a King of Arms, crowned, and a Herald or Pursuivant within the said field for making report of acts done within the same. Garter and other Kings of Arms and Heralds to be set in the scaffold before the King on the right hand, the stair of the King's 'place judicial' to make general report and to mark all that should be done in the said field. Also, [they] ordered four men of arms to be [escorts] on horseback for the departing of them, [and] when the case should require, two knights and two squires.[63]

The entering into the field the day of battle

The said eleventh day prefixed, the field so ordered and arrayed, the King sitting in his estate in his place of judgement in the field, with many noble Lords about him, great number of nobles and commoners assembled about the field, the said right noble and worshipful Knight and Lord, Sir Anthony Woodville, the Lord Scales and of Newsells etc., royally seen upon horseback, clean armed. Nine others followed him, richly trapped and seen, came to the bars. Before him [were] born two helms: The one born by the right high and mighty Prince, the Duke of Clarence, the King's eldest brother. The other, the right noble and worshipful Lord, the Earl of Arundel. The Earl of Kent, the Lord Henry of Buckingham, the Lord Herbert and the Lord Stafford, each of them bearing one of the weapons. That is to say the two spears, and the two swords.

---

[63] In practice, it seems such escorts were selected based on their suitability of rank, relative to the party they were charged to escort from the field. Thus, the specification that the men-at-arms should include two Knights and two Esquires.

The Constable and Marshall came to the barriers. Then by the King's commandment, asked the cause of his coming. The Lord Scales answered and said, to accomplish and perform the acts comprised in articles sent by him unto the Bastard of Burgundy. The King certified the same by the Constable and Marshall, commanding him to enter the field.

The King, sitting in his estate, the Lords about him, the said Lord Scales entered the field with the said nine followers, so richly seen, and came before the King's highness and did him reverence as appropriate and retreated to his pavilion set richly in the South-East corner of the field.[64]

Here follows the ornaments of the trappings of the Lord Scales, in performing his acts in Smithfield.

First. His own horse, trapped in a demi-trapper[65] of white cloth-of-gold with a cross of St. George, of crimson velvet, bordered with a fringe of gold, 1/2 foot long.

The second horse in a joust-close trapper,[66] of tawny velvet decorated with many great bells.

The third horse trapped in russet demask to the foot, powdered with two letters of his device, couched with goldsmith's work and powdered richly.[67]

The fourth horse trapped in a demi-trapper of purple demask, surmounted with a gentlewoman, girdled, enhanced with goldsmith's work [and] bordered with blue cloth-of-gold a 1/2 foot broad, and more.[68]

The fifth horse, trapped to the foot in blue velvet, the which was subtly made with pleats of crimson satin along the trapper, throughout charged with goldsmith's work, with a border of velvet upon green velvet, picked [in] gold, 1/2 a foot broad.

The sixth horse trapped in a demi-trapper of crimson cloth-of-gold, furred with fine sables and bordered a foot and a half deep of the same without.

---

[64] Although not mentioned in the details for the construction of the field, this pavilion appears to be set within the barriers. This is supported in the accounts of **AB** and **de la Marche**.

[65] Here, and in **AB** 'trapper' is used variously to refer to different forms of dress for mounts. A 'demi-trapper' is likely a half-length trapper.

[66] Perhaps meaning a trapper that is more protective of a horse expected to participate in combat with lances.

[67] The 'two letters of his device' were likely his initials.

[68] The 'gentlewoman' here is an image embroidered on the trapper, and not a rider.

The seventh horse trapped with green demask to the foot, surmounted with the attire of gentlewomen of France, charged with goldsmith's work, embroidered with russet cloth-of-gold of half a foot broad.[69]

The eighth horse trapped in a long trapper of ermines, embroidered with crimson velvet, surmounted with tassels of gold. Also on every horse, a page of his [Scale's] dressed in mantels of green velvet, embroidered with goldsmith's work, richly made. And this for the first day.

The description of the pavilion

Also, the pavilion of double-blue satin, richly embroidered with his letters; the valance thereof embroidered with his word, fixed on removable timber-work on every quarter.[70] A banner of devices, his arms in the top. A banner fixed, of his whole arms. The number of banners of the lists, beside the King's tent, on the right hand, were fifteen banners [in] rows, set on every other post of the said field, concerning the arms of divers Lordships according to the lineal pedigree of his decent, with a banner.[71]

The coming in of the Bastard

In likewise came to the barriers the Bastard on horseback, with seven followers, richly seen.

The first, his own horse, was harnessed with a rich, goodly, fashion of crimson, garnished with long swagged bells of silver, every other [one] swagged gilt.

The second horse was led before him by hand, with four Knights, richly covered with a trapper of his [Burgundy's] arms.

The third horse next following [was] trapped in a trapper of ermines unto the foot, and the reins of fine sable.

The fourth horse, covered with barding of *cour boulli*,[72] richly covered in cloth-of-gold.

The fifth horse, covered with a trapper of crimson velvet to the foot, surmounted with devise of eyes, full of tears, wrought in goldsmith's work.

---

[69] An image of a woman, as on the fourth horse.

[70] **CH** does not give Woodville's motto but **AB** quotes it as *le nonchalance*, which **CH** may have omitted for fear of interpreting it wrongly. The phrase was likely adapted from Spanish and Italianate theories on courtly eloquence and the cultivation of an effortless skill in arms or other performances that Baldassare Castiglione called *sprezzatura*. See Thomas Penn, *The Brothers York: An English Tragedy* (Penguin, 2020), e-book ed.

[71] Meaning the banners were arranged by order of precedence, around the field.

[72] Boiled or waxed leather, stiffened to act as armor (Laura Davies, "Cuir Bouilli," in *Conservation of Leather and Related Materials*, ed. by Marion Kite and Roy Thomson (Elsevier Butterworth-Heinemann, 2006), pp. 94–100.

The sixth horse was covered in cloth-of-silver, fine purple, unto the foot.
The seventh horse was trapped in green velvet, powdered with barbicans, richly made.
The eighth horse was trapped in fine sables to the foot, and the reins in ermine.
Also his pages were arrayed in joust gowns of violet color, with two pleats in white and one yellow, garnished with goldsmith's work.
The said Bastard, demanded at the porters by the King's license, entered the field with the Duke of Suffolk before him, bearing his helmet, with many noble council, [and] came before the King sitting in his estate and said 'Right high and right mighty and right excellent Prince, I am come hither before your presence as my judge in this party, to accomplish and fulfill the acts of arms contained in certain chapters to me sent by the Lord Scales, under the seal of his arms, that is here.' The King, understanding, gave him leave and license to perform it etc. Then he departed to the place where his pavilion should have been, and helmed himself openly.[73] In the meanwhile, were the spears and swords brought before the King, both counsels sent for, the said spears and swords delivered to the Bastard to have the choice of each. And so, had the proclamation made at 4 corners of the field in the form that follows:
The Proclamation
'Since it is so that the most Christian and victorious Prince, our liege Lord Edward the 4th, by the grace of God King of England and of France and Lord of Ireland, has licensed and admitted the right noble and worshipful Lords and Knights, the Lord Scales and Newsells, brother to the most high and excellent Princess, the Queen out sovereign Lady, and the Bastard of Burgundy, Count of La Roche and Lord of Beveren and Beuvry, to furnish certain deeds of arms such as are comprised in certain articles delivered to his highness by the said Bastard, sealed by the said Lord Scales with the seal and arms, for the augmentation of marshal discipline and knightly honour, necessary for the tuition of the Catholic faith against heretics and miscreants and to the defense of the right of Kings and Princes and their public estates: for so much we charge and command you, on the behalf of our most dread sovereign Lord, here present, and on my Lords the Constable and Marshall, that no manner of man of what estate, degree

---

[73] Reading **CH** gives the impression that Burgundy did not have a tent on the first day, but **AB** describes it in great detail. **CH** may have meant that Burgundy armed himself in view of the audience, rather than within his pavilion.

or condition he be of, approach the lists, save such as be assigned nor make any noise, murmur or shout, or any other manner [of] token or sign whereby the said right noble and worshipful Lords and Knights which this day shall do their arms within these lists, or either of them, shall move, be troubled or comforted, upon pain of imprisonment and fine and ransom at the King's will.'

The said proclamation made, as aforesaid, the Constable commanded a Herald to cry *'lessez aler.'*[74] And then they [Scales and Burgundy] ran a course, courageously, seeking the one on the other, which 'coup' should have been as before[75] as the Kings judicial seat was, and failed both, un-hit. And then the Lord Scales dropped his spare bevor, and *gardebras*, and the guard of his vambrace, and the Bastard dropped his also.[76] Notwithstanding, the said Lord Scales was sooner ready, wherefor he sought the Bastard further on the ground[77] and assailed him with a thrust about the neck. And the said Bastard struck with an edge stroke upon [Scales'] helmet. And the Bastard's horse's head, having upon him a chamfron, smote against the Lord Scales' saddle, and so with these strokes the Bastard with his horse, went to the ground. Then the Lord Scales, seeing him down, turned about him, holding up his sword, and then seeing that [Burgundy] could not rise, rode straight and quickly before the King, and made talk of his trapper, showing that his horse had no chamfron, nor piece of steel. And then the King commanded to take up the said Bastard. And then he came before the King. And where before the Constable at St. Pauls' it was agreed that if any horse fell, it should be lawful to his master to have another. He [Burgundy] was asked if he so would [have another horse]. His answer was that it was no sense [to do so]. Then the King commanded them to go to their lodgings.

The arms done on foot the second day.

---

[74] Indicating to the combatants that they are literally 'allowed to go.'

[75] *ferfoorth* in **Excerpta**.

[76] *Gardebras* is, according to Ralph Moffat, (*Medieval Arms & Armour: A Sourcebook: The Fourteenth Century. Volume 1 the Fourteenth Century*, (The Boydell Press, 2022), p. 373), a specifically English term for a type of shoulder defense that fit over the regular shoulder armor, called a 'paldron.' This was worn over the existing armor and held in place with a removable pin, which the wearer could remove without assistance. Likewise, the 'spare bevor' was a second plate that fit over the regular chin-guard of the helmet and an additional piece of composite armor was worn over the lower arm defense, or 'vambrace.'

[77] Meaning that Scales moved toward Burgundy who was some distance away from him in the field.

In the morning next after the eleventh day of June, before the King in the same field, the said Lord Scales, armed all save his basinet, his coat [of arms] on his back, as he did upon horseback, richly seen, came into the portal of the said field, his horse trapped to the foot in crimson velvet with seven shields embroidered with divers of the arms of his decent and one of all the whole arms, combined, fixed on the back of the said horse. The said trapper surmounted with garters richly made and bordered with fringe gold. Also there followed him eight coursers and upon [them] eight pages dressed richly in goldsmith's work. The said horses harnessed in harness of one suite. The Duke of Clarence bearing his basinet. The Earl of Arundel, the Earl of Kent, the Lord Henry of Buckingham, Lord Bourghchier, the Lord Herbert, the Lord Stafford, each of them bearing one of the weapons. That is to say, two throwing spears, two axes, and two daggers.

The Constable as before demanding the cause of his coming, [Scales] answering to perform his arms on foot in articles sent to the Bastard of Burgundy. The King certified thereof, licensed him to come into the field. He there alighting, came in before the King, accompanied with many noble Lords, doing his due reverence to his highness, [then] restored to his pavilion, richly made of velvet pally, blue, and tawney. The valance of the said tent [being of] crimson cloth-of-gold. The said pavilion being in fashion, nine squares on each corner, a banner of his arms. Upon the peak of the said pavilion, a griffin of gold, holding a banner of his whole arms. His banner held by the Clarenceux King of arms, before his tent.

The Bastard came riding to the barriers and there quickly, a worshipful company. Before him the Duke of Suffolk, the Earl of Shrewsbury, the Lord Mountjoy, Sir Thomas Montgomery, with many other Lords. Questioned at the portal of the lists by the Constable as before, by the King's license [Burgundy] entered, and came before the King, sitting in his majesty, justified the field. And there, with due reverence, showed the cause of his coming, to accomplish his second arms as before, and [Burgundy] restored to his pavilion, set in the field, in a long gown of blue velvet about him, his legs harnessed, with his arms being before his pavilion, which was of white and purple demask, pally, the peak of the said pavilion [in] gold, the valance of the said tent, green velvet, embroidered with his motto, that is to say '*null ne cy frete.*'[78]

---

[78] A Pursuivant of this name is listed among the attendants of the Duke of Burgundy listed by **CH** at the 23 May meeting in Brussels.

And in the meantime, the weapons were presented to the King, the council of both parties being present. The King beholding the throwing spears [to be] right dangerous and right perilous, in as much as it was but an act of pleasure, [he] would not have no such mischievous weapons used before [him] and commanded the said spears to be laid aside and ordered the other weapons, that is to say axes and daggers, the Bastard to have his choice, according to the articles contained in the chapter.

And then, soon after the proclamation made as before, the Constable of England visited first the Lord Scales in his tent, and found him ready. And then went unto the King, and showed that he was ready. And then went the said Constable to the Lord Bastard in his tent. And when he had so visited both, and bowed them the two Kings of Arms, the Constable then sitting in the place assigned him, the said Kings of Arms showing of them at one time to another to present their charges unto the Lords pavilions, waiting on the *lassez aler*.[79] All at one time, the King of Arms spoke these words the time of *lassez aler* now is commanded to be cried.

And then at the said King of Arms coming before the place of judgement, the King commanded the *lessez aler*. And right as the King of Arms made the cry, the Lord Scales, opened his pavilion and at the second *lessez aler* entered the field from his tent, and gave a pause, and gave countenance that he was ready with hand and foot and axe, by laying his axe on his shoulder. And then changed his axe from hand to hand.

And then they advanced and so right before the King, each assailed the other in such a way as the Lord Scales, at the counter with the point of his axe, struck through one of the ribs of the Bastard's plates, (as the said Bastard showed him after the field). And so, they fought together, the Lord Scales with the head of his axe before [him] the other with the small end, and smote many great counters and thick strokes until at the last that they fell towards a close, at which time the Lord Scales struck him in the side of the visor of his basinet. Then the King cried 'Whoo!' Notwithstanding the parting, that two or three great strokes [more were given between them], and one of the escorts staves broke between them.

And they, so separated, were brought before the King's good grace. The Lord Scales fought with his visor open, which was though perilous. The Lord Bastard fought closed, and there [before the King] opened it. And so they were brought up before the King. He commanded each to take the other by the hands and to love together as brothers in arms,

---

[79] The two Kings of Arms were Garter and Clarenceux.

which they so did. And there they immediately gave each to the other as courtesies, goodly and friendly language as could be thought. And went together into the middle of the field. And there departed each man to his lodging. Finis etc.

ANONYMOUS BURGUNDIAN

[Translated from Utrecht, MS 1117 / UBU Hs. 6 E 9, ff. 186-225, with corrections and additions from the transcription and translation of Leeds, RAR 00035, ff 44-72v by Ralph Moffat, Ralph Dominic Moffat, 'The Medieval Tournament: Chivalry, Heraldry and Reality, an Edition and Analysis of Three Fifteenth-Century Tournament Manuscripts' (unpublished Ph.D., University of Leeds, 2010), v.1, pp. 169–195, v.2, pp. 304–331]

Only two copies of this account are known.[80] Both are likely contemporary with each other and were probably composed near the time of the events they describe. The author is unknown but he was certainly a member of Burgundy's retinue and appears to be a witness to all of the events described, but does not describe any at second-hand. As a result, there is no mention of the meeting at St. Paul's on 3 June. On the other hand, the Anonymous Burgundian fills in the chronological gap between the initial issue of the challenge and the departure of Burgundy for England which is passed over by Chester Herald. This includes two diversions of Burgundy's party to combat piracy in the channel, which are alluded to in other French accounts but is unnoted in the English ones. This account appears to be aimed at a largely Burgundian audience, and one interested in the minute features of the English court. The Anonymous Burgundian gives the most detailed description of the preliminary events, particularly a mass held at Westminster Abbey, and the processions into the field of combat on the first day of the *emprise*. It concludes with a description of several events held after the *emprise* which was interrupted by the news of Duke Philips death. While this epilogue is interesting and describes a four-a-side tennis match, with a cash wager, involving the Bastard and Edward IV, it is omitted here as it contains nothing of relevance to the *emprise*.

---

[80] While the present edition of **AB** was prepared from the copy at Utrecht University Library (hereafter cited as **Utrecht**, in the notes) the transcription and translation has been checked against the Leeds, Royal Armouries copy (hereafter cited as **Leeds**), prepared by Ralph Moffat for his doctoral thesis. Significant differences between the two manuscripts are cited in the notes.

Translation

The Most Noble and Chivalrous Deeds of Arms Done in a Closed Field[81]

Since some time ago, to celebrate and glorify the most noble and chivalrous feats of arms in closed and shut field, my most re-doubted lord, my Lord Antoine, Bastard of Burgundy, Count of La Roche, Lord of Beveren and Beuvry, had carried a certain *emprise* to do feats of arms, and made this known through all the Christian realms. And to those who asked to fight him, three against three noblemen, the *emprise* had been touched by the noble and powerful lord, Sir Anthony Woodville, knight, Lord Scales and Newsells, for his third, to complete the said feats of arms.[82]

Which, nevertheless, because of the great wars and divisions which had been, both in England and in France, and other great affairs arising until death parted the said defendants, they had been unable to accomplish and perform the feats of arms. However, by certain joyous venture, which happened to the said Lord Scales, he sent to my said lord the Bastard a certain new *emprise* to do feats of arms, body for body, together with letters signed by his hand and sealed with his seal containing the chapters of the said arms to be done on horse and on foot. The manner of this event was declared by these letters most joyously and in high style. Concerning which, so that each might better understand the establishment of the said *emprise* [Lord Scales] sent to my lord the Bastard, in the town of Brussels, by Chester Herald, and which he touched with the will and consent of my most revered lord the Duke of Burgundy and of my most revered lord the Count of Charolais. I shall recite the said letters, the tenor of which follows.

Most noble, valorous, and renowned knight and most honored lord, I recommend myself to your noble and kind remembrance, affectionately and courteously, and by the greatest duty that one knight can give to another, as to one I hold myself obliged, and to be held for the great honour that on other occasions you have done me by your honourable and gracious letters and requests, showing the desire and yearning that we two might be able to assemble by arms, and the accomplishment of such a test increases the honour of nobles and augments their renown. This thing could not be put into effect until the present (to my very great displeasure) all because of the wars and divisions of this realm of England, which,

---

[81] Title from **Leeds**.
[82] This is the only account that mentions this aborted *emprise*.

from that time have lasted and multiplied, until now. Because of which I am thus legitimately excused, so that neither you, nor anyone in the world, knowing the case, can charge me or accuse me of having broken this, your noble *emprise*. But to discharge and excuse me, for God knows that the greatest desire which I have in this world is to find myself in this most honourable, and so much praised, test of arms.

And principally, so that by these means I might have the acquaintance and the friendship of you above all others of this world for the great good, the virtues, and the prowess that I know are in you, and of which your renown has been made public through all Christendom. And also, I hope that through you and your alliance I might become acquainted with, and come to know, and have communication with, the most praised and triumphant house of Burgundy of which I hold myself a most humble servant and kinsman. And which I desire to serve and honour with as much honour as it shall be possible for me to give.

These things having been considered, most honored lord, you should know that my greatest desire and my complete yearning, and will is, above all these things, to find the means to come to these aforesaid things. And God grant me such honour and grace that I might have in you the brotherhood and love of arms that two Knights can acquire and have for each other. And, to begin and have means of this noble work. I write to you to inform you of a gracious fortune which has recently come to me, asking you in all affection for the honour of noblesse and of chivalry that in this matter you give me a hearing and do me such honour as to discharge me of my obligation. And, in doing and completing this, I shall always be held and reputed your devoted Knight.

It happened that on the Wednesday after the solemn and devout day of the Resurrection of Our Blessed Savior and Redeemer Jesus Christ, for certain of my affairs, leaving high mass I approached the Queen of England and France, my sovereign lady and to whom I am a most humble subject. And, as I intended to speak to her ladyship on my knees, my bonnet from my head, as ought to be done. I do not know by which chance nor how it had come about but all the ladies-in-waiting completely surrounded me and surprised me so, that they (by their grace) attached around my right thigh a rich gold collar garnished with precious stones, and it was made like a letter which, in truth when I had perceived it, was closer to my heart than to my knee. There was an enameled flower of remembrance attached to this collar, and the flower was in the manner of an *emprise*.

And then one of the ladies-in-waiting said to me: 'Knight take this willingly for now.' And then each retired to their place. And I, completely astonished by this adventure, rose to go to thank them for their rich and honourable present. And as I went to put on my bonnet, which I had let fall close to me, I found in it a bill of writing, sealed and closed, with only a little gold thread. Therefore, I knew well that it was the contents of the will of the ladies, in writing, and that which I must do and accomplish for the noble remembrance which they had given me.

Then I most humbly thanked the Queen who (by her grace) had suffered to have done me such honour in her noble presence. And similarly, I thanked the ladies who had given me this noble present, and I went straight to the King of England and France, my sovereign lord (as ought to be done) to relate to him my adventure and show him the *emprise* with which I had been charged. I showed and gave him the bill close, beseeching him in all humility, that it might please him to do me such honour and grace, to consent and agree to the will of the ladies in this party, and that he might give me consent and license to accomplish the contents of these letters, granted to me, to complete the adventure of remembrance. By his grace the King broke the gold thread and had the said letters read containing certain chapters, which pleased me greatly, and of which the tenor follows.

Here follows the chapters

In honour and reverence, and aid of our blessed savior Jesus Christ, of his glorious Virgin Mother, and of my lord Saint George, the vary tutor, patron, and cry of the English, for the augmentation of chivalry, to the commendation of noblesse, and for the glorious school and practice of arms, and the valor that I can maintain and ensure with all my power, and to obey and please my fair lady, I Anthony Woodville, Knight, Lord Scales and Newsells, Englishman, have today, the 17th day of April 1467, received from the ladies the gift of a rich gold collar and, hanging from this, a noble flower of remembrance which (by their grace) they have attached and placed on my right thigh.[83] By the favor, pleasure, consent, and license of the King, my sovereign lord, I have charged and taken this flower of remembrance for an *emprise* to complete and accomplish (with God's help) the feats of arms which follow.

Firstly[84]

---

[83] Here **AB** accidently gives the date as 1467 as later notices correctly date events to 1465.
[84] Sub-heading not in **Leeds**.

Item I shall be held by express command to appear in the noble city of London on the day and hour which shall be set and ordered for me in the month of October, next coming, before the King, my sovereign lord, or his deputy as my judge in this party, against a nobleman four lineages and without reproach, of my choice, if he will present himself against me.[85]

The second chapter is such that we shall come together on horseback, each armed at his pleasure, in saddles of war, without rests of advantage or malign devises, and we shall run only one course with the lance without a barrier, with sharpened spear points. And then taking sharp-edged swords in hand, and we shall fight either with the point or edge, to the advantage of each, until the accomplishment of thirty-seven strokes with the sword, by us both.

The third chapter: I shall provide lances and swords, which my companion shall have the choice.

The fourth chapter is that should it happen (which God prevent) that one of us two be carried to the ground, out of the saddle, without the horse being borne to the ground by a blow of the lance or sword, the feat of arms shall be considered accomplished.

The fifth is; If one of us two is injured (which God prevent) either by the lance or sword, to the extent that he is unable to complete, the feat of arms shall be deemed accomplished as above. And that is all for the first feat of arms.

Here follows the second [feet of] arms

Item: I shall be obliged to present myself for the second time before the King, my sovereign lord, or his deputy as my judge in this party on such day as shall be assigned to me in this month of October against a nobleman of the aforesaid condition, if he shall present himself against me to do, complete, and accomplish the feats of arms which follow.

The second chapter is that we shall be armed on foot as is suitable for noblemen in such a case, and may carry shields and pavises at the choice of each, and we shall be armed with spears, axes, and daggers, and shall have only one cast of the spear. Then we shall fight with the other weapons until one of us two is forced to the ground, or disarmed at all points.

The third chapter, is that I shall provide the said weapons, of which my companion shall have the choice.

And that is all for the second feat of arms

---

[85] **AB** does not correct the October date for the *emprise* as given in **CH**.

And should any question or debate arise or be caused by these present chapters, by there having been badly couched, badly written, or badly understood, one can be sure that the King will order for this cause such notable men that the differences will be quickly settled protecting the honour and the right of all the parties.

And for conclusion of these present chapters I shall be held at my expense to have made and obtained from the King my sovereign lord sure, legal, and sufficient safe conduct for the noblemen who shall do me such honour as to come to fight me, according to the contents of my chapters, to be able to come, stay, and return safely, and without malignity in this realm of England, as well as other lordships belonging to the King my sovereign lord, for such a time, and such a term, as they shall ask, and with such number of men and horses as they shall conveniently require, and is appropriate to such a case.

Most honourable lord, by these present chapters, you see and understand the charge by which I am obliged and held under the will of the ladies, and that I am bound by their command, and they wish that I should do these feats of arms in this city of London, and in this realm of England. And this thing I cannot disobey, remove myself, or infringe, therefore to complete and accomplish that which I have been ordered and the contents of these present chapters for the discharge of my burden, to sate my long desire, and to appease my heart of its desire, and for the great and reasonable causes motivating me as I have written presently here above, I send to you, to ask in all affection and cordiality, Chester Herald, servant of the King of England and France, my sovereign lord, to present to you, from me, these letters and present chapters, together with the most noble flower of remembrance, which has been granted to me and charged as an *emprise*.

I beg and ask you (if you please) to show me such honour and friendship as to touch the said flower, my *emprise*, and to accomplish the feats of arms contained in these present chapters. I have sent this flower across the sea to you as the most renowned Knight, and the most ready, and appropriate, to accomplish such noble works without blame whom I could have chosen or identified by advice or request.

And always I bind myself and my possessions and whatever by good fortune God will grant me to be yours as far as honour, life, and possessions can suffer for this. And when the said Herald, officer of arms, bearer of this aforesaid *emprise*, shall return to me and shall have reported to me that the said flower has been honored and touched by so worthy and chivalrous a hand as yours, then the said flower shall joyfully be retaken by me and I shall wear it as my charter and the cause from which I hope to pick more fruit, and honour, in this world.

And I shall wear it so, until the time that I shall have completed and accomplished these present feats of arms against you, most honourable lord, because I understand that to such a high and noble person as you many affairs may continually arise and many interruptions to your high undertakings such as by civil wars arising in your borders, accident of illness, the will of your sovereign, or the pleasure of your lady; which is not to be disobeyed. And so each one of these problems may be suffered by all noblemen and to you and others it is a legitimate and reasonable excuse to delay many high and honourable emprises.

In consideration of this, to show to you the honour, the desire, and the affection which I bear for you above all Knights, I have thus asked and have obtained that if it should be so, that by one of these reasons or some other legal excuse, you cannot come to do or uphold the accomplishment of the said *emprise* nor complete the feats of arms which I ask of you in the month aforesaid, I shall await you and bear the burden of my charge for a whole year starting from the end of the month of October up to the date of one year having expired. That is to be understood that all the time during the time of this year I shall be obliged within two months of summons before the day of our first combat that it will have been notified to me the place, day, locality that shall be set for you and with appropriate judges to fulfill these feats of arms according to the contents of my chapters. And so, I promise that unless a reasonable cause occurs which is worthy of my excuse then I shall do and accomplish the contents of these chapters.

And let no one suppose that I do or undertake the aforesaid things out of arrogance, presumption, envy, or excessive self-confidence. For, by God and on my honour, I do them only to obey my fair lady and to have the acquaintance of the merit, principally of a good Knight for which you are my choice. The creator of heaven and earth, to whom I pray, knows this full well, and may God grant you joy of your lady.

Most honored lord, most noble, valorous, and renowned Knight, so that you shall be made more certain [of what] I wish to undertake, do, and accomplish, the aforesaid things, I have sealed these present chapters with the seal of my coat of arms and signed them by my hand in the place and royal manor of Sheen, on the 18th day of the month of April, one thousand, four hundred and five.

Thus, my Lord the Bastard, desiring to satisfy these letters, received them as is said. But, with the will and consent of both parties the feats of arms were always suspended and, in particular, because of the expedition of France where [Burgundy] was engaged at the encounter at Montlhéry and the expeditions of Liège and Dinant until this present year, [1467] when things found themselves settled, so that my Lord the Bastard left the town of Bruges on the 24th day of the month of April accompanied by a great number of knights and squires the majority of whom I shall very soon describe, and went to Sluys to wait for wind in order to sail to England to the town of London where Lord Scales was awaiting him to complete the contents of his letters, as it shall be hereafter related.

Nevertheless, the wind was such that it was not suitable to make this voyage until the 18th day of May, which was the Monday of Pentecost. And always my Lord's household remained at Sluys and he in his own person went to Our Lady of Ardembourg, and was personally present at the procession of Bruges which was held on the 3rd of May.

And it came about that during this trip one day my said Lord was in his ship when some Basque pirates took an English carvel and brought it, full of cloth, to anchor at the point of Sluys. Hearing news of this, my Lord the Bastard sent two of his carvels forward to take them and bring them back. He had four of these carvels to undertake his said voyage. The captains of these were of the first [carvel] (in which was my said Lord the Bastard) James de Boschuse. Of another, James de Dausset, my said Lord's master of the household. Of another Fierin Palesding, Captain of my Lord's archers. And of the fourth, Gerard de Hoccon, Bailiff of Lille.

And so, my said Lord sent the said James de Dausset and Fierin Palesding to take these Basques, and their prey, and they brought them in, and my Lord delivered them into the hands of the Bailiffs of Lyane and of Sluys to do what should be done by reason of justice.

Here follow the names of the knights and squires who accompanied my lord the Bastard, of which I protest, in putting them in writing one first, then another, as I remember their names, without regard to their precedence at all. And so, I pray that in this I shall be deemed excused.

Firstly:
Sir Simon de Lalaing, Lord of Montigny
Sir Philippe, Bastard of Brabant Lord of *Rombyque*[86]
Sir Claude de Toulongeon, Lord of La Bastie[87]

[86] Philippe is so styled in **Utrecht**, but is named only as The Lord of *Crubeque* in **Leeds**.

[87] Lieutenant of the marshal of Burgundy and would be a judge at the *Pas* of the Golden Tree, 1468 (Baker-Grant and Damen, p. 256 n.).

My lord of Montferrant[88]
Sir Jehan, Bastard of Wavrin, Lord of Forestel[89]
Sir Pedro Vásquez[90]
Sir Philippe de Gohen
Sir Jehan de Chassa, Lord of Monnet
Sir Jehan de Rombrettes, Lord of Thiebaultville
My lord D'Antreulles
Sir Josse Vassenart
Here follow the squires without household offices:
Philippe Bouton
Gerard de Rousillon[91]
Gerard de Hccon[92]
Claude de Blesy
Father Peter
Charles de Toulongeon, Lord of Traves
Hugh de Lanoy
Pierre de Lanoy
Antoine Duzies
Philippe de Salins
Pierre de Salins
Etienne Chatars
John de Banst
Jacques de Tinteville
Claude de Vaudrey
Boudoin de Croix[93]
Pierre Mettenes
John le Tourneur[94]

[88] Perhaps a relation of Blanche de Montferrat, dowager Duchess of Savoy.
[89] It is possible that this is the chronicler, Jehan de Wavrin, whose account appears below. If so, he would have been of an advanced age, having fought at Agincourt, and living to 1474 (de Wavrin, *A Collection of the Chronicles and Ancient Histories*, vol. I, pp. vi–ix). He also accompanied Simon de Lalaing and others on an embassy to Rome, on behalf of Philip the Good, in 1463 (Baker-Grant and Damen, p. 407).
[90] Pedro Vásquez de Saavedra was an experienced tournier and had fought a single-combat with Richard Woodville, Anthony's father, in 1440 (Baker-Grant and Damen, p. 73).
[91] Competed in the *Pas de La Fontaine des Pleurs* at Chalon-sur-Saône, 1449–50 (ibid., p. 166).
[92] Entered as *de Occon* in **Leeds**.
[93] *de la Croix* **Leeds**.
[94] This seems, literally, 'John the Tourneyer'.

Pierre de Cressy
Allan de Marcenelles
Hugh de Scoemies
Antoine, Bastard of Aussy
George, Bastard of Aussy[95]
Philippe de Carrin
Kemart Dolehan
James le Noble
John de Sue
Achilles de Flessin
Hugh Moureau

Here follow the squires, bearing the paid offices of 'the stool' and the stables:
Jehan de Dausset, master of 'the stool'
William de Cressy, clerk of the pantry[96]
Hugh Cocquet, cup bearer
John de Maupas, first squire of the stables
Allan Bournel, second squire of the stables
Louis de *Werquingnoel*, marshal of the lodgings
Jehan de Lonchamp, squire of the kitchen
Massin Prevost, comptroller
William de Rogierville, greeter[97]
And Morlet de la Haye, receiver general

Here follow the archers:[98]
Fierin Palesding, squire, Captain of the archers
Gerard Mainborde, archer
Le Luffre, archer
Savarot, archer
Thomas de Villers, archer
Guy le Jeusne, archer
Martin Baron, archer
Bartholomew Widoque, archer
Pierre Haresque, archer
Arnold Poullet, archer

---

[95] Not in **Leeds**.
[96] Speculative reading of *Pannetier*.
[97] Speculative reading of *Sourrier*.
[98] In this context, the archers act as bodyguards and grooms, or militarized servants.

Pierre du Castel, archer
'Brigade', archer
Hannequin Martin, archer
Mailinet Denis, archer
Here follow the other officers of the household:
Gerard Mainborde, usher of arms
Jacques de Marques, called 'the Doctor,' usher of the chamber
Casselaire master of tax
'Little Guy' *potagier*[99]
Florecon and *Mahiot*, wine steward and *saucerie*[100]
Amandin, wine steward of the pantry
Troctet fruiterer
Denis, saucier
And all the companions serving in the offices
The Chaplains:
Item. The first, \Master/ Antoine de Terni, doctor of theology, and six others following.
And other ministers to the number of 12:
Golden Fleece, King of Arms
Burgundy Herald
Fusil Herald
Limbourg Herald
Namur Herald
And La Roche Pursuivant
Here follow those of the chamber:
The Bastard of Naus, wine steward of the body
The barber
The squire
The tapster[101]

Item. Armorers and saddlers, and a great number of valets, amounting in all to more than four hundred people.

And so, accompanied by a great quantity of servants, on Monday the 18th day of May, at the hour of ten in the morning, my Lord left and joyfully passed the day until around the hour of seven in the evening when my lord halted the ships toward night, to wait on several little ships from

---

[99] A cook with a specialty for soup.
[100] Sauce maker.
[101] Attendant in charge of beer, or drinks other than wine.

Flanders, Zeeland, England, and other parts that were all nearby. Then my said Lord and his company saw five good carvels of Spanish pirates and thieves come toward them. The pirates took the wind to attack us and immediately my Lord and his men took sail and came against the Spaniards, as did an English ship which was in the company, and such exploits were done that the said Spaniards jumped on us, and we on them, that is by missiles hurled by powder[102] and by hand, with very great diligence on one side and the other, without us being able to board them because of the dark. And[103] that they kept a good watch, and the skirmish thus lasted until around the hour of ten, when they retreated scarcely far from us, for in the morning we could clearly see them.

There was, in a little ship that accompanied us, one man killed by a crossbow bolt to the head, in another, a man was lost overboard, and in another, a man who had his leg shot off by an iron fowler, from which [wound] he died.[104] Of the Spaniards, no one knows what losses they had suffered. However, in the morning at around the hour of ten, they made for the coast of Flanders and they left us. The wind was against us, and thus it was Thursday before we reached the coast of England and Saturday before my lord could go \to London/. And so, because I had time and leisure and on the information of the sailors, I put in writing the places of the coast of England of one bank and the other of the Thames up to London in the manner of a pastime.

First, in the open sea one passes on the coast toward France a very fair and grand island called the *Isle of Thanet*, where there is the entrance to a good village called Margate. Then there is Reculver, then, entering the Thames, one passes on this same side a place called Queenborough where there is a convent near a Minster on *Sheppey*.[105] Item: a village called Cliffe.

[102] **AB**'s literary description of gunpowder weapons, as opposed to bows.
[103] And 'also' in **Leeds**.
[104] *veuglaire* in **Utrecht** and **Leeds**. The term was commonly used in English legal records as a generic name for any gun, but is most often translated as 'fowler', a type of gun popular for birding and usually loaded with several projectiles or 'hail-shot' (see Ralph Moffat, *Medieval Arms and Armour: A Sourcebook. Volume II: 1400-1450*, (Boydell Press, 2024), p. 197 and Dan Spencer, *Royal and Urban Gunpowder Weapons in Late Medieval England* (Boydell Press, 2019), pp. 243–5).
[105] **AB**'s unfamiliarity with English is clearer in this passage as many of the place names are written out phonetically, from heavily accented French or Flemish. Thus, Thanet is rendered *Tend*, Margate is *Marguate*, and Queenborough is *Kennubrouc* (**Utrecht**). **AB** was also confused by the fact that the location on Sheppey is called *Minster* rather than the place being 'a' Minster.

Item: Gravesend. On the other bank toward the north, entering the Thames, is Wakering and a castle and a great borough called Hadleigh.[106] Item: leaving Gravesend, from which it is only twenty miles to London, one passes on one bank of the fair river and on the other Tilbury, Northfleet, Winbrech, Saint Clement, Dartford, Aveley, Thurrock, Barking convent, then Greenwich, which is the King's house three short miles from London.

On Saturday the 23rd day of May, at an hour after midday, before Greenwich, came [to] my Lord the Bastard, a noble Knight called Sir William [sic.] Tiptoft, Earl of Worcester, Constable of England, in a fair *fust*, or galleon, with sixty oars, and five barges \full/ of the most important Londoners with several little ships who all attended my said Lord and sailed with him. And then they came to one mile from London and they joined him [Burgundy] and the said Constable and all the others did him reverence. Then the said Constable took my lord in his *fust* and the five barges took all of our people from the ships and joyfully led the company up to London Bridge.[107] There my Lord disembarked, then he and the Constable mounted ponies and went right through the town to the Bishop of Salisbury's residence where my said Lord lodged himself.

The King had this residence hung with his tapestries and, in the cellar, had placed eight barrels of wine, although my said Lord had brought a hundred barrels and more. On Sunday the 24th of May my Lord the Bastard went to hear mass at Saint Paul's Cathedral, holding and showing his estate. And he was so accompanied by the Lord of Flanders, Sir Pierre de Mirammont, my Lord of Rabodanges, and Master Andrew Colin, President of Flanders, who had been in London a for some time, on an embassy of my Lord the Duke of Burgundy.[108]

After returning from Saint Paul's, where my Lord was seen by many people, he treated to dinner the said ambassadors, and on this same day at supper, the Bastard of Brittany came to visit him whom he feasted similarly.

On Tuesday the 26th day my Lord the Bastard went away from London to wait in private at a place three miles away from there called Chelsea. And in this place, he waited until he came to do his feats of arms.

On the 29th day of May the King of England came secretly to the place of Chelsea to visit my Lord the Bastard and he only had my Lord Hastings,

---

[106] **AB** does not record these locations in the literal order in which the flotilla passed landmarks as Wakering is located directly North of the Isle of Sheppey. The Hadleigh mentioned here is to the West of Southend-on-Sea, and has little significance other than, one assumes, the personal interest of **AB**'s informants and is a speculative reading of *Calghie* in **Utrecht**.

[107] **Utrecht** gives us the creative phonetic attempt at his title of as *Deluourcestre*.

[108] Likely Claude de Rabodanges, Lord of Thun (Baker-Grand and Damen, p. 265 n.).

Great Chamberlain, the Earl of Essex, Grand Master of the Household, John, Lord of Buckingham, Lord Rivers, Sir James Douglas, Sir Thomas Auburn, and Sir Thomas Montgomery in his company. And my Lord the Bastard had summoned from London my Lord of Montigny, Sir Philippe de Brabant, Sir Claude de Toulongeon, Sir Pedro Vásquez, my Lord of Monnet, my Lord of Thiebaultville, and Philippe Bouton to accompany him. The King did not want my lord the Bastard to come out of his residence so he waited around eight feet inside the door and there he did reverence, and the King very humbly received it. Then they took a turn in the garden and the two of them spoke for a good half-hour. And, at the end, the King called Lord Rivers and these three spoke for a time, then they were presented with wine and spices in the residence. And so, the King left and returned to Windsor where he was in residence.

On the next to last day of May the Duke of Clarence, the King's brother, came to this place of Chelsea to visit my Lord the Bastard, accompanied by my Lord the Constable. On the 2nd day of June my Lord the Bastard went to London to see the entry of the King who entered his city very grandly accompanied by the nobles of England, each so arrayed as to their estate. And so, carrying the sword before him, was Lord Scales, who brandished and flourished it very proudly, when he passed before my lord looking up at him as he was at a window.

On the following third day my lord the Bastard went toward the King in fair estate accompanied by all his knights, gentlemen, and archers. And he was conducted to Westminster by my lord the Chamberlain up to the King's chamber where the King came and then received him publicly. And, after reverence had been done by one side and the other, my Lord the Bastard had the King assign the day for the accomplishment of his feats of arms. The King granted him the choice of day, which he named, and which the King accepted as Monday the 8th day of the month. But then, at the request of my lord Scales, because it was raining and the field was soft and sunken, the day was to be delayed from Monday to Tuesday, and from Tuesday to Thursday which was the eleventh day of the month. At this point, when the day had been agreed, the King began this day to hold a general parliament of all the realm, where it was the custom in such case to solemnly celebrate a mass of the Holy Spirit where the King came in royal estate and all of those who were obliged to come to this parliament were called to it.[109]

[109] Edward IV had issued writs of summons for a parliament in February, 1467 to commence on 3 June. On the 10th, it was informally prorogued until the 15th (*PRME XIII*, p. 250).

The King of England came to the mass of the Holy Spirit in Westminster Abbey dressed in a cloak of crimson velvet with a royal chaperon round his neck furred with gray fur[110] with headdress made from crimson velvet with a big head band[111] covered with gray fur, having with him the following Dukes and Earls; that is: the Duke of Clarence, and the Duke of Suffolk, the Earl of Arundel, the Earl of Worcester the Constable, the Earl of Kent, who carried the King's sword before him, Earl Rivers the Queen's father, the Earl of Essex Steward of the Household, the Barons Audley, Zouche, [and] Hastings King's Chamberlain, that [Lord] Berners [the] Queen's Chamberlain, and those [Lords] of Howard, Stafford, Sandwich, Cromwell, Herbert, Scourton, Montjoy, and Yvain. All these Dukes, Earls, and Barons were dressed in royal cloaks like the King except that they had on the right shoulder, from the breast to the back, bends of gray fur as wide as a palm. The Dukes had four, the Earls three, and the other Barons two. The Archbishop of Canterbury, who sang [the mass] was also at this mass with the King. And the Bishops of London, Rochester, Ely, Norwich, and of Lincoln, and the Abbot of Westminster. Also, the King carried a scepter in his hand which is said to have been Saint Edward's.

Also, my Lord the Bastard was at this mass with the King throughout, and went before the King in the procession of the bread and wine. And after the mass my Lord the Bastard went with the King to a room in the palace where the Bishop of Lincoln made a long speech to open the parliament. And my lord was thus always present near the King. And the speech having finished, he returned the King to his chamber where he took his leave and returned to his residence in London, then once more went to Chelsea until the time he had to come and perform his feats of arms.

On Thursday the 11th day of June, 1467, in the marketplace of London, was a park made with a double list of one hundred and eight paces long, and seventy-two wide. At the middle of one side was the entrance for my Lord the Bastard and, on the opposite side, that of my Lord Scales. On the east side there was a high platform made for the King which was grand and spacious, hung with silk cloth the color of blue, sprinkled with gold fleur-de-lys and with scrolls where it was written 'Forever.' In the middle of the platform was a tall chair covered with rich cloth-of-gold and stuffed with cushions of the same.

[110] *Letuce*, in **Utrecht**, referring to the winter fur of a species of weasel.
[111] *Bourrelet*, being a wrapped band of fabric, like that worn under a helmet as padding.

At the base of this platform, on two sides of the steps, were the seats of the Constable and of the Marshal, hung and adorned with tapestries. And above the said Constable, who was on the right, was the place of the Kings of Arms and Heralds. Opposite the King, on the other side of the field, was a stand for the Mayor of London and his people and, near him toward the south, a stand for the people of my Lord the Bastard. And all around the field stands were erected and most of the houses' windows were open.[112]

On this said day around the hour of 8, the said Constable and Marshal came to the field with a great following of men-at-arms and archers carrying *vouges*, swords, or axes. The Constable's men all wore the same white clothes, some with goldsmith work, and the others without. And the Marshal's men wore vermilion with a little lion on the front and back.

And you should know that the Marshal was a Knight named Sir John Howard, in place of the Duke of Norfolk, who is the hereditary Earl Marshal. The said Constable and Marshal's themselves, were arrayed in leg harness, gorgets, and tabards. The Constable's of cloth-of-gold and the Marshal's of goldsmith work. And [they were] mounted on trapped horses. The Constable's of crimson cloth-of-gold and the Marshal's of blue and violet silk, strewn with loops of hanging silk.

So, they smartly led their men between the two lists: the archers and the men-at-arms against the pillars of the field throughout on this first day. But on the following day they had them enter between the two lists on foot, and each retired as was right and was customary.[113]

At one corner of the field at his end Lord Scales had pitched a pavilion of azure taffeta, strewn with embroidered silver letters which were 'm's and the border at the bottom was embroidered with his motto, which was in ancient letters, in white on blue velvet [and read] '*La non chaillance.*' And there was a gold eagle holding a banner of his coat of arms on this pavilion and eight banners encircling this pavilion, and banners around the field on his side, of which there were 43 in all. Twenty-three different, one from the other, showing all those from whom [Lord Scales] is descended, and others of his wife's ancestry. He showed on the first banner the arms of Saint George, [the arms of] Woodville, Rivers, Priaux, Baux, Limbourg,

---

[112] **AB** refers to the private houses facing into Smithfield. In mid-fifteenth-century London, Smithfield was already surrounded by built-up areas, most conspicuously, the complex belonging to the Augustinian priory of St. Bartholomew, mentioned in Chester Herald.

[113] This describes the 'double lists' which formed two cordons around the field, with a space between the two barriers where these men were posted (see the description given above in **CH**, from Stow, *A Survey of London*, vol. I, 32–3).

Luxembourg, Enghien, France, Bonnecie, Châtillon, Geneva, Athens, Brienne, Belzigat, Scales, Nucelles, Beaufort, Lille, Dowic, Beauchamp, and Conversano. Thus was the field ordered, completed, and prepared.[114]

The King came, accompanied by the nobility and by his guard behind his platform, to enter within between the hours of nine and ten, on account of the press of people, and was dressed in a short robe of black velvet, with violet hose, and the garter on his left leg. Then, after a while, when he was ready, came my Lord Scales in this manner.

My Lord Scales was accompanied by the Duke of Clarence mounted on a horse trapped with blue cloth-of-gold, very richly bordered with a gold fringe and black silk, and [he] carried in his hand an armet garnished with precious stones. After him came the Earl of Arundel also carrying an armet or helm, his horse trapped in crimson cloth-of-gold, bordered with ermine on white cloth-of-gold, and the said border was covered with a silk veil. Lord Rivers' horse was trapped in white cloth-of-gold, bordered with marten, and a Knight named Sir Laurence Rainsford had a horse trapped in blue velvet strewn with little footed cross-crosslets of gold embroidery and with a great number of bees, as were his brothers and the other Knights and Squires who accompanied him. Lord Scales had trumpeters and minstrels before him. Then he had the lances and swords carried on horseback before him, and of his estate he was in order as follows.

His body was armored, except for his head, and his horse was trapped with white damask with great crimson velvet crosses of Saint George. And the horse was gray. He had eight pages after him dressed in black satin pourpoints, having mantelets with green satin sleeves strewn with white goldsmith work, and caps fashioned like bird's beaks,[115] of brown both bordered with black velvet, with silk veils entwined around the top. The first horse was trapped in tawny velvet with gilt bells. The second with ermine. The third with violet velvet strewn with goldsmith work fashioned like the clasp of a lady's girdle. The fourth was of gray velvet bordered with white cloth-of-gold with his letters [as above]. The fifth with

---

[114] While the association of some of these arms with the Woodville's is clear (Rivers, Scales, Newsells), most of them are derived from Earl Rivers' wife Jacquita (Beaufort, France, Luxembourg).

[115] *et chappeaulx a facon de bicoques*. Also spelled *bicoquet*, this was a felt cap with a pointed brim. The name was also used to describe a type of helmet with a tall crest, but context here favors the felt version (E. J. Lewandowski. *The Complete Costume Dictionary* (Scarecrow, 2011), p. 30).

cloth-of-gold called 'false Bourget'[116] bordered with ermine. The sixth with green satin, all strewn with lady's headdresses and long veils. The seventh with blue velvet, with great hangings of goldsmith work fashioned like eight teardrops together with long robes. The eighth was of crimson cloth-of-gold, bordered with marten. And in this manner, he came to do reverence to the King.

After a path had been made for him [Lord Scales] onto the field by the Heralds, he paraded around it, then he dismounted and went inside his pavilion, and his horses were led before the field on his side. Lord Scales dismounted and, his head completely uncovered, he remained at the entrance to the pavilion until he had seen the entrance of my Lord the Bastard in this manner as shall be said hereafter.

After the arrival of the appellant Lord Scales, my Lord the Bastard came in such order as follows.

Firstly, his archers came two by two, dressed in their tabards, without halberds or staves. And after them came the master of the household, alone, gripping his baton. Then, afterwards came the gentlemen in twos, after them the Knights and each knelt before the King in passing, then there followed trumpeters and Heralds. And my said Lord came after accompanied by the Duke of Suffolk, Lord Montjoy,[117] and by Sir Thomas Montgomery,[118] who had been sent by the King to do this. And the said Duke of Suffolk had a great company of men all arrayed in white taffeta or satin, and he himself was mounted on a horse trapped with fine crimson cloth-of-gold.

My Lord the Bastard had led before him a horse trapped with the arms of Burgundy with the bar [of difference], this horse was led by four Knights of his company. And he himself was mounted on a gray [horse] with a hanging harness, half cloth-of-gold, and half cloth-of-silver, strewn with half-silver and half-gilt bells. And six Knights of his company led him by hand. Then he had seven horses trapped very richly. The first with ermine. The second with green cloth-of-gold. The third with crimson velvet with big silver eyes which were all strewn with teardrops. The fourth with crimson cloth-of silver-bordered with green velvet. The fifth had a bard covered with fine gold brocade. The sixth with sable marten. The seventh with blue velvet strewn with embroidered barbicans of fine gold.

---

[116] *bourget faulx*.
[117] Walter Blount, 1st Baron Mountjoy, former treasurer of Calais.
[118] Keeper of the royal mint to 1466.

2 THE SOURCES   63

His pages and one palfrey-man rode these horses arrayed in green satin pourpoints, cloth-of-gold caps, lined with black velvet on their heads, having blue and violet damask tabards bordered with yellow silk fringes.

In this manner did my said Lord, very richly, enter the field at the entrance to which the Constable and Marshal came to fetch him with a great number of officers of arms of England wearing crowns on their heads and long rods in their hands. And so, there was the King of Arms of Rome, and that of Denmark. And on our side Golden Fleece of Burgundy, the Heralds Limbourg, Namur, Fusil, and La Roche Pursuivant. And of England, Richmond, Rivers, Newsells and many others, all of whom conducted my Lord before the King.[119] To whom my said Lord did reverence, his head bared, all on horseback. Then he took himself to his side where he had a wooden mounting stand, for helming, and for arming with the helm, and the *pieces* which were carried in two leather containers, onto the field.[120]

My said Lord the Bastard did not yet want to put on his helm until he had first seen the lance and sword with which he had to fight. Of these the said Constable and Marshal, when Lord Scales had sent them to be presented to the King, then gave my lord the choice.

Then he put on his helm, in the midst of the field, and in such manner that the said Constable and Marshal retired to their seats, and that Richmond Herald cried in English at the four corners of the field, the customary cries. These having been done, Garter King of Arms cried three times: '*Laissez les aller!*' Then Lord Scales left his pavilion, lance couched, and my Lord the Bastard took his lance on his thigh and charged at him. And so, they came to meet, but they did not meet at all. Although my Lord the Bastard kept his course very well, targeting Lord Scales. The course of the lance having finished, the two knights suddenly disarmed themselves, most handsomely, of their lances and their additional armor.[121] Lord Scales [discarded] two, and my lord the Bastard, four. And then they came swinging their swords very proudly. Lord Scales twice cried out loud: 'Saint George!', and my Lord the Bastard, who was on the nearer

---

[119] This is the second, and final, mention of a Pursuivant named *Nucelles* who is otherwise undocumented.

[120] This would typically be read as 'coins' or currency, but this is the first mention of any cash prize, or the like. Therefore, its meaning in this context is uncertain until it appears again, further in the text.

[121] Here, the significance of the *pieces*, is made clear—these are additional pieces of armor, worn for the running of the lances, but discarded before continuing combat with swords.

end, if he had wanted, turned his horse's head (without using his hands) toward his man, and dealt him a stroke with his sword on the helm. It was so strong that afterwards it could be seen on Lord Scales's helm, on the side of the visor that had been split, was three inches wide, and a grain of wheat could pass through the gap.[122] By this stroke, the sword was fractured in two places.

And they met so hardily that my said Lord the Bastard's horse was seriously injured not only its head, but its body, and the bit in its mouth. Thus, when the second sword stroke was dealt, the said horse fell on its haunches, then fell completely, and rolled over on my said Lord the Bastard, who still held up his arms and sword, until the King had the said horse lifted off him. This horse, its saddle and bridle having been removed, rolled over five or six times, stumbling on weak legs, then lay there spraying blood in very great abundance. And the following day it died in the Heralds cordon. Then they found a great hole there in the throat as if from Lord Scales sword. It [was as if it] had a dagger inside its mouth; none knew if this was true. Nevertheless, it died as is said.

My Lord the Bastard went before the King, asking to perform the 37 sword strokes, but the King, as judge, declared the feat of arms on horseback as done, and accomplished and ordered the feat of arms on foot to be held the next day. Although it was the case that the King had my said Lord questioned, asking if he wanted to perform the feats of arms on foot and, when he had answered yes, he did not want to allow it at all.

On the following day, which was Friday the 12th of June, the great and sumptuous estates returned in place. The said Constable and Marshal did their duty in the morning to put their men in order. A pavilion had been pitched for my Lord Scales which was paly with blue figured satin and tawny velvet above. And below was blue and tawny velvet with a border of crimson brocade cloth-of-gold. And the banners were the same as the day before with a very great banner on a lance planted before this pavilion.

My Lord the Bastard also had a rich pavilion pitched which was paly with white and violet damask with a rich gold pommel, the banner of Burgundy on top with a border of green velvet embroidered with gold barbicans and with his motto 'None shall touch me' and initials in large

---

[122] In other words, the crack in Scale's visor was the inches long, and the gap in the crack was wide enough that a grain of wheat could pass through it. Note that other selections of translation have rendered this as an 'ear' of wheat. So this was a gap between perhaps 2–10 mm.

forms. And also, there was the great banner of Burgundy before this pavilion held by a Herald.

The King came at about the hour of 11, as he had done the day before, dressed in a short gown of crimson cloth-of-gold. Before him, the young Duke of Buckingham and his brother, and the other Lords who have been named above. For everyone was serving, such that there was no one of note left at court. And when the King had come, my Lord Scales came a very long time later, his body armored, dressed in his coat-armor, accompanied as above.

And so, he was on horseback and as follows. The horse on which he came to the entrance of the field was trapped in crimson velvet embroidered with eight shields of his lineage, and, on the haunches a great shield of his coat of arms, and all strewn with garters. And seven pages came dressed in crimson satin pourpoints with blue satin tabards, bordered with pointed black cloth strewn with white goldsmith work of Lord Scales's letters. On their heads they had tawny velvet caps with white plumes, and each had a horse harnessed with a large harness of crimson cloth-of-gold. Taking the banner placed before the pavilion and carrying it before him in this manner, his men came before him and, after them, came trumpeters and minstrels.

The Constable and Marshal presented him to the King to whom he did reverence and then he retired to his pavilion. And it is not to be forgotten that he had carried before him the throwing spears (which were nothing but javelins, equipped in the middle with crimson velvet), two axes with cutting edges and rondels,[123] and two short daggers.

Immediately after my Lord the Bastard came on horseback to the barrier, his men came before him in order as the day before; his pages were on foot. After them came the archers dressed in violet camlet with two teardrops of his livery. These teardrops were strewn with gilt and white goldsmith work. My Lord the Bastard was dressed in a long robe of blue velvet furred with ermine. He had come to be fetched as the previous day before the Constable and Marshal and officers of arms and presented himself to the King in very great honour. Then he retired to his pavilion and each retired to his place. The cries were made as they armed themselves. And

---

[123] Meaning circular hand-guards mounted below the axe-heads, intended to protect the users' hands from weapons running down along the haft from the head (see the late fifteenth-century example at Leeds, Royal Armouries, object number VIII.1542, which retains its rondel below the head).

the Knights of each side went to receive the weapons of which my Lord of Montigny and Sir Pedro Vásquez made the choice for my said Lord.

But it was the King's will that the said spears or javelins were not to be thrown as (it was said) the ladies had requested it. In so doing the King asked my Lord who answered that he wished to obey the King's will, also that they would carry nothing save for axes and daggers. Six armed guards remained in the field as well as the noblemen who had done feats of arms in the past who are named hereafter.

All this having been done and ordered, the cry was made '*Laissez les aller*!' And so, my Lord Rivers, three times, made the sign of the cross over his sign, and Lord Scales left [his pavilion], his axe sometimes at his neck, sometimes in his hand, where he held it on high.

And my Lord the Bastard, similarly carrying his [axe] with confidence before him, advanced against him until he was a little way beyond the King. There they came against each other very chivalrously. And my Lord Scales shouted to my Lord the Bastard in a certain manner shouting 'Hey, over here, over here!' And my Lord the Bastard answered with these words 'These words dismay me not a whit unless you come closer!'

Then, without waiting at all, or hesitating to answer, Lord Scales forced the point of his axe into the Bastard's visor. But my Lord the Bastard dealt the first stroke to his breast with the [bottom] end of his axe. Both of them were very violent, and the noblemen said that they had never before seen such hard axe strokes.

With one stroke my Lord Scales lost his axe from his hand [but] soon regained it. And the two of them fought so valiantly and so forcefully that none knew who was best. Except that I know well, that from the place that they began my Lord the Bastard had gained ground advancing on him, and was continuing to do so, when the King cast down the baton. Then the guards were placed between them.

But it was with great difficulty that Lord Scales was made to stop. As soon as 'whoa!' had been cried, my Lord the Bastard had stopped, but not my Lord Scales who, while in the hands of the guards, dealt him some strokes, as a result of which my Lord the Bastard was forced to deal him such a powerful stroke with the axe-head to his head, and did so with such force, that he was master of them, who most valiantly showed themselves to have had the power to have well sustained [the blows].

It appeared too, in my lord Scales' coat-armor which was torn in several places. And my Lord the Bastard had, in particular, the third plate of his harness, at the bottom, broken right away.

Having finished the combat, they raised their visors and, taking each other by the hand, went together before the King; my Lord the Bastard on the right side of Lord Scales. And doing reverence to the King and thanking him, they made very gracious offers of friendship to each other.

And so, the King deemed the feats of arms accomplished for both days and they were declared to have completed the honour of each of the two parties. So, each left amiably and retired to their lodgings. After the champions had been disarmed and a little refreshed, at some time between the hour of three and four, they went before the King. Lord Scales went first and waited for my said Lord the Bastard on Westminster Bridge and they went together to the King who held for them a very great feast especially for my Lord the Bastard, because he was a foreigner.

And, after the reception, they took part in, and played at, tennis four against four. That is the King, my Lord the Bastard, Lord Scales, and the Marshal against Sir John Woodville my lord Scales' brother, Sir Thomas Auburn, Thomas *Vacquant*, and my lord of *Rabodangers*, Bailiff of Saint Omer. And neither side won. And so, others began to wrestle until it was night when my Lord the Bastard took his leave and returned to his lodgings.

On Saturday, the day was occupied with the feats of arms of my Lord of Monnet which were done on foot this day and the King was present at them. On Sunday after dinner my Lord the Bastard, as he had not yet seen the ladies, went to the palace where they were all assembled with the Queen in a richly decorated room. And, from the entrance of the porch, up to the end where the Queen was before a high hung seat, it was all full of ladies on one side as richly arrayed as possible. Some in gold, the others in silk.

My lord the Bastard and all the nobles who so wished to advance their honour were gently kissed by the ladies and entertained with fair words, some speaking French and the others not. And those who did not know how to speak were obliged to make signs each to their ability. Then the time came to leave to go to a very noble banquet that the King had had prepared in London at the hall of the Grocers which was the most appropriate place of all to do this. Each came down from the palace and all the Lords and Ladies went aboard barges and came by the river ashore in the middle of London where horses for the Lords and hackneys for the Ladies were waiting for their passage. And so each mounted and with great joyfulness came to the said place.

The great hall of this residence was hung with entirely new rich tapestry of gold and silk that showed the Siege of Jerusalem according to Josephus. On the left-hand side of this room was a high cabinet with four shelves most richly garnished with gold and silver dishes such as pots, cups, ewers, 'drageoirs,' and bottles. Three tables were dressed in the said room and, on the right, opposite the cabinet, was a chamber hung with the same cloth of which I have spoken above, that with which the platform of the King was hung in the field. In this chamber there were three tables also dressed and covered, without a cabinet. And above this chamber was another chamber where two tables were covered.

When the King, the Queen, my Lord the Bastard, and all the company had come, and when the meal had been finished, the King led them into the garden which was marvelously pleasant. The dance began there. The King danced, and the Queen, and all the others in their turn. Also, there was constructed in the middle of the park where they danced a pavilion made of briar where eight players were enclosed, who played very melodiously with lutes and *gitterns*.[124]

When it was time for supper the dance finished, and the King came to eat in the said low room which was above this garden; and my Lady Margaret, his sister, next to him at the end. And the Queen was at the other end, next to my Lord the Bastard. But, because she was pregnant, she did not stay long but soon retired. And so my Lord the Bastard, my Lady of Exeter, my Lady of Beaufort, and the elder Lady Buckingham remained there at table. The other Ladies and Knights and gentlemen, both English and ours, were at the other tables. In the said room the Earls of Arundel and Worcester were at a low table, and the tables were all completely full of Knights and gentlemen both theirs and ours. Lord Scales mixed similarly at the high table and my Lord the Great Chamberlain [Lord Rivers] was at the third table. My Lord the Bastard's pages were next to him. The officers of arms after, and then all my Lord the Bastard's archers and some archers of the Crown. In the said high chamber were the damsels and a few men with them. The supper was long and I would have taken pains to describe all these ladies, but had it not been for Lady Scales who promised me, by her grace, to give me in writing, as she did, all those of whom the list follows:

---

[124] A stringed instrument similar to a lute (Mary Remnant, "Medieval Fiddles, etc." *Early Music*, 5, no. 2 (1977): 255).

Firstly
The Queen
The Duchess of Exeter
The Duchess of Suffolk
Lady Margaret
Other duchesses:
The Duchess of Bedford
The Dowager Duchess of Buckingham
The Duchess of Buckingham, sister of the Queen
Lady Anne, niece of the King[125]
The Countess of Richmond
Baronesses:
Lady Mautravers
Lady Bourchier
Lady de Veer
Lady Beaumont
Lady Gray
Lady Scales
Lady de Strange
Lady Berners
Lady Stanley
Lady Hastings
Lady Clinton
Dames:
Lady Catherine Strangeways
Dame Alice Fogge
Dame Joan Norice
Dame Joan Dareth
Dame Elizabeth Odale
Dame Anne Chamberlain
Dame Elizabeth Darcy
Dame Margaret Raleigh
Dame Joan Westmarch
Mistress Strange
Mistress Clinton
Mistress Hastings
Mistress Dunne

[125] Anne Holland, wife of Thomas Grey, Queen Elizabeth's son by her first marriage.

Mistress Prout
Mistress Halkett
Mistress Howard
Mistress Taveran
Mistress Gherninghan
Mistress Gainsford
Mistress Newton
Mistress Belknap
Mistress Harcourt
Mistress Vendhan
Mistress Croxforde
Mistress Malpas
Mistress Moresby
Mistress Haulte
Mistress Wvrege
Mistress Ede
Mistress Boudon
Mistress Norbery
Mistress Denton
Mistress Westmarch
Mistress Hartwell
Mistress Preston
Mistress Percy
Mistress Croxton
Mistress Gedding
Mistress Loys
Mistress Mille
Mistress Denholm

So, supper passed, garnished with Lords and Ladies. Then they went to dance for a very long time. The King danced some more and the Queen [too]. And, the dance being over, spices were carried in on seven very rich dredgers of both gold and silver, and wine flowed in great abundance. The King left and the Ladies came as far as the river where my Lord the Bastard took his leave and the King retired to Westminster.

On Monday the feat of arms on horseback of my Lord of Monnet was done after dinner and we were there until the hour of 11. Philippe Bouton and Thomas de Lalande were meant to do their feats of arms on the Tuesday, but the King delayed it until the Wednesday, and went to the archers' garden after dinner where my Lord the Bastard was to shoot. Then, when the company left, he went to the Duchess of Exeter's residence where she held a banquet for the King, the Queen, and for my Lord the Bastard. All the oft-named princesses were there, and the Countess of Northumberland who had newly arrived. And, if the feast had been joyous on Sunday, it was no less so on Tuesday.

On Wednesday at around three hours after dinner the King came to Philippe Bouton's feat of arms on horseback for which the whole day was needed because of a [lance] rest, that Thomas de La Land wore was too advantageous. The King was so angry about this that he would not be happy until my Lord the Bastard dismounted from his horse and begged the King's grace for this Thomas, to which he consented.

The feat of arms having finished, my Lord the Bastard gave to Lord Scales, and delivered in the field, a horse called 'The Hart.' To Sir John Woodville he gave another roan horse, which was most noble, and to the King a bay [horse] on which he was mounted. The King, of his grace, immediately mounted it and returned on it for the day to Westminster.

[Here follows a description of a tennis game involving the Bastard and Edward IV, a description of a feast, and the unexpected news of the death of Phillip the Good, precipitating the Bastard's departure.]

OLIVIER DE LA MARCHE *MÉMOIRES*

[Translated and edited from Olivier de La Marche, *Mémoires d'Olivier de La Marche, maitre d'hotel et capitaine des gardes de Charles le Téméraire*, ed. by Henri Beaune and Jules d'Arbaumont (Librairie Renouard, Henri Loones, successeur, 1883), vol. III, pp. 41–42, 48–57]

Olivier de la Marche (1425–1502) was a career soldier, courtier, and royal administrator for the Dukes of Burgundy and later, Emperor Maximilian I. He was also an accomplished author and amongst his works is the sprawling *Mémoires* which includes this eye-witness account of the *emprise* at Smithfield.[126] This account is more candid than the previous two, paying more attention to some of the actions and disputes over the running of the *emprise* and the character of the participants. De la Marche is also interested in the other combats held around the main event, and

---

[126] Marco Nievergelt, 'The Quest for Chivalry in the Waning Middle Ages: The Wanderings of René d'Anjou and Olivier de la Marche.' *Fifteenth-Century Studies* 36 (2011), 137–67.

names several individuals and another controversy that emerged from one such combat. While de la Marche was definitely present at the *emprise* he was not there as part of the Burgundian party, but was already in London on separate business. Because he was a close intimate of the Bastard of Burgundy, his account benefits from his detailed knowledge of the parties involved and his privileged access to Burgundy's retinue. This account also mentions the factional crisis that kept Burgundy from keeping the original October date for the event. Known as the war of the league of the public weal, the Bastard was involved in several actions, including the siege of Liège.[127]

There is no complete and accessible English translation of Olivier's *Mémoires*, therefore, the present edition is a translation of the 1883 French edition by Beaune and d'Arbaumont.[128] As with the other editions and translations, I have standardized the spelling of personal and place names. Grammatical structure has been adjusted for readability, where needed, but when the meaning would otherwise be obscured, this is left untouched and notes are provided to explain confusing passages. I have kept the paragraph breaks as they appear in Beaunne and d'Abaumont.

Translation

At this time the Lord Scales, brother of the Queen of England, gave a challenge of arms on foot and on horseback, and made known to my Lord the Bastard of Burgundy that, if he would take up this challenge, and relieve [Lord Scales] of his charge, he desired it before all others. My Lord the Bastard who, of course, had asked to take up arms and fight in an enclosed field, was very happy with this news, and brought it to the Duke, his father, who generously granted him to accomplish this feat of arms against the brother of the Queen of England and thus was this challenge

---

[127] Vaughan, *Philip the Good*, pp. 380–91.

[128] An English translation was prepared by Dorothy and Georgina Stuart c. 1930 but this exists as a single typescript held in the British Library, London (Olivier de la Marche, *The Memoirs of Messire Olivier de La Marche*, ed. by Dorothy Margaret Stuart and Georgina Grace Stuart (c.1930), shelf-mark 09073.e.3). The account of the 1468 *pas de l'Arbre d'ore* is translated in Andrew Brown and Graeme Small, eds., *Court and Civic Society in the Burgundian Low Countries, c.1420–1530* (Manchester University Press, 2007), pp. 54–85. My thanks to an anonymous reviewer for this reference). Accounts of other *pas d'armes* recorded by de La Marche are translated in Baker-Grand and Damen, pp. 72–9, 152–84.

accepted. And each prepared at his own cost, what was needed and Phillipe Bouton and Jehan de Chassa prepared to take up arms and accompany him to England.[129]

[A lengthy description of the events surrounding the league of the public weal, and its aftermath, that occupies the Bastard in 1465, before returning to the preparations for the *emprise* in 1467]

These things done, the Duke sent his natural son to England, well supplied with all things; and there [with him] was [Sir] Simon de La Laing as his chief guide, Sir Claude de Toulongeon, lord of La Bastie Sir Philippe, Bastard of Brabant, Sir James de Montferrant, Gérard de Roussillon, the Lord of Thiberville, and several others. And at this time, I found myself in England and stopped to see these [deeds of] arms, and certainly, the Bastard of Burgundy held such a bearing and such triumph, as could be done by a legitimate, eldest son of Burgundy. But let us keep quiet about these things for present, to talk about the execution of these arms.

King Edward of England had prepared a large and splendid list, and for his person, was made a very large and very spacious lodge, and the floors of this house were made in such a way that one climbed by degrees up to where the King was. He was dressed in purple, with the garter on his leg, and a thick baton in his hand, and truly he appeared in character, worthy of being King, because he was a handsome Price and grand and well mannered. An Earl held the sword before him, a little to one side. And around him were twenty or twenty-five elder councilors, all white-haired knights who resembled senators counseling their master. The Earl of Worcester took the place as Constable and was accompanied by the Marshal of England, and well he knew how to do his job.

On descending from [the King's] hoarding (there were three hoardings)[130] on this side [of the field] and beyond of said degrees. In the first were knights, in the second were squires, and on the third archers of the crown, each with a *voulge* in his hand.[131] And at the foot of the said

---

[129] Both men are listed among those accompanying the Burgundian party in **AB** and their combats are alluded to at the end of **CH**, although Phillipe is identified as *Ernalt*.

[130] *Hourtz* in **de la Marche**, which translated literally would be closer to 'hoarding' like the frontage of a building. Here he is referring to temporary structures, like the *maison* of the King which function as viewing platforms for the different groups.

[131] Henri Beaune and Jules d'Arbaumont translated *voulge* as 'dart', perhaps thinking these were carried as a mark of their status. It is more likely this was meant to be *veuglaire*, a type of early firearms usually called, in English, a fowler (Spencer, *Royal and Urban Gunpowder* pp. 243–5).

steps [to the King's house] were two pulpits, one for the Constable and one for the Marshal. And at the opposite side of the list, was one 'house' not so high as the King's, for the mayor of London and his alderman and servants for that year.

And sometime after the King was seated on his throne, which was very nice to see, the Mayor of London accompanied by his Aldermen and those of the King, entered into the list, the sword in front of him, and drew before his 'house' and passing before the King, and showed no deference until kneeling down, the Mayor and all the others, and put the point [of the sword] down as a sign of humility, and then quickly got up. And the Mayor of London went to his hoarding, as ordered for him, and abode there to see the feats of arms, having always the sword before him.

And only the guards of the lists, namely eight well-mannered men-at-arms well mounted and armed made their entry into the said lists, by the Constable's leave, who ordered them to do as they would have done. Sometime after Lord Scales came to the entrance of the lists, and the Constable went to meet him and asked him his questions. He [Scales] replied that he came to present himself before the King of England, his sovereign Lord, to make and accomplish the arms that he had made against the Bastard of Burgundy, and thereupon an overture was made to him [Scales], and of course he was richly mounted and armed, and had ten or twelve decorated and richly dressed horses. And after his presentation made before the King, he withdrew to a small tent which was ordered for him.

And shortly afterwards came the Bastard of Burgundy, who similarly asked for entrance, which I observed was granted. And the said Bastard presented himself in front of the King to provide arms. And you must know that he was very sumptuously dressed, and had twelve horses, some clothed in cloth-of-gold and others in velvet, charged with bells and others covered in martens, which one calls sables[132] which were as beautiful as it was possible to find. The others were covered with embroidery, lavishly made. The pages were dressed the same, as it needed, and certainly it was a rich company, and whom the King accepted willingly. His presentation made, he [Burgundy] withdrew into a small tent made for him.

And quickly the cries and trumpets were made, as accustomed, and, carried before the King by two Earls, were two lances, and two swords, of

---

[132] Sable ermine.

one [the same] style and grandeur (because the Lord Scales' by his chapters, must deliver the arms to the choice of the opposing party) and the King sent the said weapons to the Bastard of Burgundy to choose what suited him the best.

The Bastard of Burgundy chose fairly lightly, and the two weapons were held in the hands of two officers-at-arms who kept them outside the pavilion until it was ready to emerge. And after cries and ceremonies made, the champions were seized their spears and swords, ordered for them.

And they put their spears into arrest, and ran a course without making or sustaining [any blow] against the other. But on the return, they made [contact] when they took swords in their hands the horse of my Lord the Bastard struck his head against the horn of the saddle of the Lord Scales and of this blow the horse killed himself, instantly, and fell with my Lord the Bastard under his horse, sword still in his hand.

And soon after this the King of England rose up, and he [Burgundy] showed himself very angry with the Lord Scales for that he should claim that there was false devise of his horse, but none was had, so it happened that this blow was made to the horse by misadventure, as I have described. And the King gave them leave for this time, and my Lord the Bastard returned to his lodgings, and he said to me, on returning to his room, 'Don't you worry, he [Scales] fought a beast today, and tomorrow, he will fight a man.'

And at this time came the Constable from the King, to know if he was injured. But my Lord the Bastard answered, that he thanked the King and that he had no injury but that he was ready the next day to perform his arms on foot, praying that it was the King's will to grant it.

And the next day at the appointed hour, appeared in the camp my Lord, the Bastard and my Lord of Scales, and as always, the Duke of Suffolk accompanied my Lord the Bastard, and cordially accompanied him.[133] And after the cries and ceremonies were made, Lord Scales sent three types of weapons to present to the King for the performance of these feats of arms on foot, and for the Bastard of Burgundy to have the weapons of his choice. The first two were throwing spears, and they were carried by two knights. The second weapons were two axes, carried by two Barons. And the third weapons were two daggers, carried by two Counts. And when the weapons were presented, the King kept in his hands the two

---

[133] John de la Pole, second Duke of Suffolk (1442–1492).

spears and the other four weapons were sent by them to my Lord Bastard to make his choice according to the contents of the chapters [of the challenge]. And the remaining weapons were brought by the Constable to Lord Scales. And then came the footmen, namely six men-at-arms, well appointed, each holding a wooden baton in their hand.

The Bastard of Burgundy was dressed with his coat of arms of Burgundy with a bar across, for to show that he was a bastard.[134] And the Lord Scales bore his coat of arms also, and carried his axe on his shoulder, like a pike, and came, shouting 'Saint George!' three times.

The champions joined proudly and assaulted each other in great courage, and it was a very beautiful battle. Never did I see axes fought so proudly and certainly my Lord the Bastard showed well in that battle that he was a man, a knight studied in arms and a master. And both were taken and parted, one from the other, without much hurt. And thus were these feats of arms accomplished. And in truth, I have seen from the harness of Lord Scales where Lord the Bastard had made great cuts with the bottom point of his axe, and as for the daggers given them, they did not themselves use them in this battle.

And so, the champions took the command of the King, and parted all at once, their axes on their shoulders to show that they had not been disarmed, and each withdrew to his lodgings. And at the regard of the King of England, they had supper prepared in the hall of the Mercers, and there came the ladies, and you will certify that I saw there sixty or eighty ladies of such noble houses that the least was the daughter of a Baron and was most rich and plenteous, and my Lord the Bastard and his people feasted grandly and honestly.

And the next day were performed arms on foot by Sir John de Chassa and a Gascon squire named Lois de Baces, servant of the Lord Scales, and these deeds were accomplished without a great crowd.[135] And the next day were deeds of arms on horseback, which Sir John de Chassa had the greater honour and was held to be a good runner of the lance. And the

---

[134] In heraldry, marks of 'cadence' were added to arms to identify heirs and here a similar mark of difference, a 'baton sinister' is indicated for a natural son of the holder of the arms (see the distinction between the baton and bend in James Dallas, "The Bend Sinister," *Notes & Queries* 7th series, vol. IV, Nov. (1887), pp. 401–2).

[135] Jehan de Chassa, Lord of Monnet, who was also challenged through ornate correspondence, by Louis de Bretelles, esquire who is here named Lois de Baces. An account of their combat is appended to the Leeds copy of **AB** but is not reproduced here.

next day a deed of arms was performed by Sir Phillip Bouton against a King's squire. That squire was a Gascon named Thomas de la Lande.[136] This Thomas was a handsome companion and good man. And between them they whispered a question, because those who served Sir Philip Bouton said that the hold of Thomas de la Lande was too advantageous. It was observed by the people of the King and found that it was true, which the King was not happy with. However, they condescending to practice their arms and each did the best that he could, as is customary in such a case, and thus were the arms completed on the one hand and on the other. [...]

JEHAN DE WAVRIN'S CHRONICLE

[Translated from Jehan de Wavrin, *Recueil Des Chroniques et Anchiennes Istories de La Grant Bretaigne, a Present Nomme Engleterre: Volume 5, from A.D. 1447 to A.D. 1471*, ed. by William Hardy and Edward L.C.P. Hardy, Rolls Series (Eyre & Spottiswoode: London, 1891), pp. 543–4]

Wavrin (or Waurin, c.1400–c.1474) was an illegitimate son of a French noble and compiled a lengthy chronicle which extended into his own times, ending in 1471. A 'Jehan, Bastard of Wavrin' appears in Anonymous Burgundy's roster of Burgundy's entourage and it is entirely possible that this is the same man. While nothing in this account contradicts the claim it was made by an eyewitness from within Burgundy's retinue, it is so brief that the proximity to events seems irrelevant. This lack of detail may suggest that Wavrin was little interested in these events or was too much occupied with other duties to take much interest in them. It is worth noting that Wavrin does not mention Scales' relationship to the Queen. Rather he mentions only Anthony's father, Earl Rivers, who was also Edward IV's Chamberlain at the time. Somewhat like the account from *The Great Chronicle of London*, Wavrin worries he is not up to the task of narrating the combats themselves and excuses his brevity by skipping to the unwelcome news of the death of the Duke of Burgundy.

---

[136] Scofield, *Edward the Fourth*, vol. I, p. 419 identifies this as Thomas de la Lande (or Launde) who married Katherine, daughter of Lord Wells. Lande was executed for his participation in the July 1469 uprising in Lancashire (ibid., pp. 509–10).

Wavrin's chronicle was edited for the UK Records Office *Rolls Series* with five volumes in the original French, but only the first three volumes were translated into English, which only reached 1431. This edition is, therefore, a translation of the French version from that series.

Translation

And elsewhere, Sir Antoine, the Bastard of Burgundy, passed over the sea and entered the Thames, in the City of London, where he was honorably received, and feted. And he had a great abundance of nobility in his company, for he had set a day between him and Lord Scales, son of the Lord Rivers, to take up arms. Which were only two [namely] on horse and on foot which were accomplished most notably, of which I must be brief. And it would have been a most pleasant feast if not for the news arriving of the death of the noble Phillip, Duke of Burgundy.

Enguerrand de Monstrelet's Chronicle (Continuation)

[Edited from Enguerrand de Monstrelet, *Chronicles of Enguerrand de Monstrelet [...]*, Thomas Johnes ed., (London: Henry G. Bohn, 1853), vol. I, p. 345]

Monstrelet was a bureaucrat and chronicler from Picardy (c. 1400–1453) who composed a detailed account of French and international affairs, modeled on the more famous work of Jean Froissart. Monstrelet's own work was expanded by later continuators up to 1516 and therefore the account of the *emprise* must be a pastiche of contemporary or near-contemporary accounts, and not a direct eye-witness record. The mention of the hostile pirates encountered by Burgundy's flotilla suggests that it was either influenced by the account of the Anonymous Burgundy, or that this episode was more widely known in French-language circles. However, this account merges the two separate incidents into one, during which Burgundy seizes two ships from his attackers. This account articulates great disappointment that Edward IV intervened to stop the combats. The implication is that witnesses from Burgundy's party expected more from the fights, but that the English believed the goal was simply to entertain the King.

Translation

Soon after Easter, in the year 1467, Sir Antoine, Bastard of Burgundy, crossed over to England, to perform a deed of arms against the Lord Scales, brother of the Queen of England. He went thither handsomely attended by warriors and artillery; for there were reports which proved true, that there were some pirates on the seas lying in wait to defeat him, under the pretense of being Spaniards, although they were French.[137] It happened that the Bastard's men took two of these vessels, richly laden and full of soldiers, which were plundered, and then he arrived safely in England. He performed his deed of arms greatly to his credit; but it did not last long; for as it was done to please the King of England, he would not suffer the combat to continue any time, so that it was rather for amusement.

Gregory's Chronicle

[Adapted from *The Historical Collections of a Citizen of London in the Fifteenth Century*, ed. by J. Gairdner, Camden Society, New Series (Camden Society, 1876), p. 236]

One of several chronicles written by, and for, a London audience, this chronicle was once attributed to William Gregory (mayor of London 1451–2) but his death in January 1467 means he cannot be responsible for this account of the *emprise*. Whoever the writer was, they confess that they were not a direct witness but only describe what was told to them by those that did. What is said is fairly general although more attention is given to the events of the third day, including names of the English and Burgundian combatants.[138] Embree and Tavormina argue persuasively that the continuator of the chronicle was a Londoner who had knowledge and experience of warfare, and took great interest in events touching the same. Sadly, his account of the combats here are rudimentary.[139]

---

[137] **AB** calls the Pirates Spanish and Basque. No other account suggests they were French.
[138] The current theory is that the chronicle was compiled by a succession of authors, without any one major contributor. Dan Embree and M. Teresa Tavormina, eds., *The Contemporary English Chronicles of the Wars of the Roses* (Boydell Press, 2019), pp. 3–4.
[139] Ibid., pp. 11–12.

Transcription

Also, the same year there was deed of arms done before midsummer in Smithfield between the Lord Scales, the Queen's brother, and the Bastard of Burgundy, both on horseback and on foot. But I know not what I shall say of it, whether it was fortune, craft, or cunning, but this is a truth, that the Bastard of Burgundy lay in the field, both horse and man, and his horse was so bruised that he died within a while after. Then the next time they fought on foot full well. I report what was said to me by him that saw this. Or, ask of them that felt the strokes. They can tell best. Also, that same time there was deeds of arms done between 2 Gascons of the King's house and other 2 men of the Bastard of Burgundy. And the 2 men in the King's party, their names were Thomas de la Land and the other Louis de Bretails [sic.] and that other 2 men in the Bastard's side, their names were Sir John de Casis, [sic.] Knight, and the other Buton, Squire.[140] But the King's men here better than they both on horseback and on foot. And these deeds of arms were for life and death. And so, it was between the Lord Scales and the Bastard of Burgundy.

COTTON MS VITELLIUS A XVI

[London, British Library Cotton ms Vitellius A xvi, f. 126. Transcribed from *Chronicles of London*, ed. by C. L. Kingsford (Clarendon Press, 1905), p. 179.]

This anonymous chronicle is part of the literary corpus of London chronicles and shares the same interests and many common sources as others, including Gregory's Chronicle. Less personal than Gregory's, this account focuses on the success of the English participants (or, those representing the English) rather than the details itself, or even the noble audience. No mention is made of the incident with the Bastard's horse, or the intervention of the King on the second day. It is a straightforward report of aristocratic activities for an urban, parochial, audience with only passing interest in the sporting life of this most international city.

Transcription

Also in this year in June were certain acts of war and jousts done in Smithfield between the Lord Scales and the Bastard of Burgundy. Whereof

---

[140] This is Louis de Bretelles mentioned in **de la Marche** (as de Baces).

the Lord Scales had the honour. And that done, where other points of war done between certain gentlemen of England and diverse servants of the said Bastard. Whereof the Englishmen had the worship.

LAMBETH MS 306

[London, Lambeth Palace ms 306. Transcribed from *Three Fifteenth Century Chronicles*, J. Gardiner ed. (London: Camden Society, 1880), p. 92.]

This short passage is not actually part of the chronicle preserved in this volume (a late fifteenth-century chronicle in English which ends in 1464). Rather it comes from a notice written on the inside cover. James Gardiner attributed it to the sixteenth century, based on the scribal style. It is otherwise anonymous but does not obviously follow previous descriptions suggesting it is a copy of an original (rather than derivative) account. Once again, the special interests of different witnesses are represented here with the detailed description of the twice-enclosed field and its costs. It is worth comparing this description to that in **CH**, **AB**, and **de La Marche** with this one, and the surviving financial accounts that or the formal accounts for the construction of the *emprise* lists that survive in the National Archives.[141]

Transcription

The lists that Anthony Lord Scales and Anthony the Bastard of Burgundy jousted in, in Smithfield: the timber and workmanship there cost 200 marks and were of six of the thriftiest carpenters of London, bought and made. The length 26 taylors yards and 10 feet, 24 of breadth and 10 feet, double-barre: the inner bars were much greater than the outer and between both [the distance] 5 feet. The jousts began the Thursday next after Corpus-Christi day, anno domini 1467 and in the 7th year of King Edward the IV, Thomas Howlgrave, Skinner, being Mayor of London.

---

[141] These are Kew, National Archives E 101/474/1 (a 14-leaf manuscript of accounts for the event) and is discussed, with other similar records, in Sydney Anglo, "Financial and Heraldic Records of the English Tournament," *Journal of the Society of Archivists* 2 (1962), pp. 183–95.

Howard's Chronicle

[Oxford, Bodleian Library Ashmole MS 845 f. 21v. Adapted from "Herne's Fragment" in J.A. Giles, ed., *The Chronicles of the White Rose*. (London: James Bohn, 1843), p. 18–9.]

Thomas Howard, 2nd Duke of Norfolk, was a son of one of Edward's household retainers and as such, served the King as a teen and went on to serve in the court of Burgundy from 1467–8. The Howards were beneficiaries of Richard III's largess and the Howards rose with him John Howard becoming the new Duke of Norfolk in 1483. That ended with the coming of Henry Tudor and the death of Richard III at Bosworth. John Howard died there as well and his son Thomas was wounded. He survived his wound and the settling of scores by the new regime. In time the family gained the trust of Henry VII, if not their former fortunes, although Thomas was restored to the Earldom of Surrey. His participation in the English victory at Flodden earned him the title his father' held so briefly. It was in the years following 1522 that he seems to have dictated his memoirs to a secretary who was responsible for the fragment that survives.[142]

This account was, for many years, known only by the name of its first editor, Thomas Herne, who transcribed and published it in the eighteenth century. The manuscript Herne copied was thought long lost until MS Ashmole 845 was identified as the source in 2009.[143] This discovery confirmed that the memoir was that of Thomas Howard whose account of the *emprise* is therefore an eye-witness account. However, clearly Howard's memory was no longer crisp when recalling events after a passage of more than 50 years. The chronology is confused (Howard places it in Edward IV's 7th year, not his 5th, and after Charles' succession as Duke, rather than before). He mentions only the combat of the second day, without showing any awareness that there was any other combat between the two. Clearly, the ferocity of the combat he did see impressed him as his admiration for the skill and energy of the axe combat did not fade with the rest of his memories. Given how much combat Howard did go on to witness, and participate in, over his long career in arms, his assessment of this combat is worth examining.

---

[142] Embree and Tavormina, pp. 19–21.

[143] D. Morgan, "Herne's 'fragment' and the Long Prehistory of English Memoirs," *The English Historical Review* 124, no. 509 (2009): pp. 811–32.

Transcription

In this year and in the month of June, then being the 5th year of King Edward, Antoine, Bastard of Burgundy, came to England with diverse others from the Duke Charles of Burgundy to threat for a marriage betwixt the said Duke Charles and Dame Margaret, sister of King Edward, the which was concluded.

After this was great triumph made. Most especially in Smithfield were jousts. Whereas the said Antoine, Bastard of Burgundy and Anthony Woodville, Lord Scales and brother of the Queen, with diverse others, ran diverse days, and those 2 before-named fought on foot with axes as men courageous and greatly expert in those feats of war. And this done, the said Bastard returned to Flanders with many great gifts etc.

THE GREAT CHRONICLE OF LONDON

[Adapted from A. H. Thomas and M. A. Thornley (eds.), *The Great Chronicle of London: Guildhall Library MS 3313*, (George W. Jones: London, 1938), p. 203–4.]

The Great Chronicle of London was long attributed to Robert Fabyan, a London draper and alderman (d. c.1512) who certainly did prepare a chronicle but probably not this one.[144] The surviving manuscript (London, City of London Corporation, Guildhall MS 3313) may be based on first-hand accounts of events from 1440 onward but this is not certain.[145] Whatever the source for the account of the *emprise* it does appear to be an original one, as it does not show any features from previous accounts. It does ascribe the death of Burgundy's horse to some object attached to Woodville's mount. The description of the foot combat on the second day is also different than previous accounts. This does briefly mention the combats that followed on the third day, carefully noting that the English were generally successful.

This is the first notice to claim that Burgundy's horse was 'blind'— meaning that it was either blinkered or had some degree of vision

---

[144] M-R McLaren, 'Fabyan, Robert (d.1513)', *Oxford Dictionary of National Biography* online ed. (OUP, 2004).

[145] C. L. Kingsford, *English Historical Literature in the Fifteenth Century* (Clarendon Press, 1913), p. 77, 99–104.

impairment (natural or artificial) that contributed to the injury it suffered. This is a detail that many later accounts include, suggesting it became a popular source for writers who had access to English sources. The edition given here is taken from the 1938 edition of Thomas and Thornley. It has been silently modernized.

Transcription

[...] In this mayor's time, and the month of June were certain feats of arms done in Smithfield between the Lord Scales, brother unto the Queen, and the Bastard of Burgundy, whereas were present the King and Queen and most of the great estates of this land. Where the first day they ran together with sharp spears, the which course they finished to both their honour, and that done to each of them was delivered a sharp sword to tourney with. And so, they ran together with eager mood, the Bastard sitting upon a bay courser, being blind, and the Lord Scales sat upon a grey courser which was well decked for war. And upon the piece of harness, standing upon his nostrils, has fastened a sharp pike of steel, the which [was the cause] of a casualty, as the horses met, and turned, struck the blind horse so sharply in the nostrils that with pain of the stroke, he mounted so high that he fell with his master in the field. And when he was so overthrown the Lord Scales rode about him with his sword shaking upon him until the King called to the Marshall and such as had the rule in the field to part them and to help the Bastard upon his horse again. And when he was again horsed, he made fierce countenance to have assailed his adversary. So that day was finished to the Lord Scales honour.

Then upon the morning the said 2 champions met again in the said place where they fought on foot with axes. But the fight continued not, for after 3 or 4 strokes at the most, the King cast down a warder which he held in his hand and commanded them to be separated. And so that day was ended indifferently of honour.

Then upon the third day, were certain points of war there executed between certain gentlemen of England and servants of the said Bastard's, among which many sore stripes were given and received. But the lauds of the days tourney was given to the Englishmen.

Chronicle of Robert Fabyan

[London, British Library Cotton MS Nero C xi, f. 416. Adapted from Robert Fabyan, *The New Chronicles of England and France: In Two Parts*, ed. H. Ellis, (London: F. C. & J. Rivington; T. Payne; Wilkie and Robinson, 1811), pp. 655–6.]

This chronicle was definitely the work of Robert Fabyan, and comparison of this account with *The Great Chronicle* notice shows enough differences in the substance of the account to make the argument that the two descriptions must have used different sources, although they do agree on the spike mounted to on the chamfron of Woodville's horse. Otherwise, Fabyan gives a different reason for the King cutting the second day's combat short. Fabyan's work gained much wider circulation than earlier chronicles thanks to the efforts of Richard Pynson who printed the chronicle in 1516.

Transcription

[...] And in the month of June following, were certain acts and feats of war done in Smithfield, between Anthony Woodville, called Lord Scales, upon one part, and the bastard of Burgundy, challenger on the one part; of which the Lord Scales won the honour. For the said bastard was at the first course running with sharp spears, overthrown horse and man, which was by the rage of the horse of the said bastard, and not by violence of the stroke of his enemy, and by a pike of iron, standing upon the fore-part of the saddle of the Lord Scales, wherewith the horse of the bastard being blind, was stricken into the nostrils and for pain thereof mounted so high upon the hind feet that he fell backward.

Upon the second day they met there again upon foot, and fought with their axes a few strokes. But when the King saw that the Lord Scales had advantage of the bastard, as the point of his axe in the visor of his enemies' helmet, and by force thereof was likely to have borne him over, the King in haste, cried to such as had the rule of the field that they should separate them, and for more speed of the same cast down a warder which he then held in his hand. And so were they parted to the honour of the Lord Scales for both days.

Upon the morrow following and the other days were certain acts of war done between diverse gentlemen of this land and certain of the said bastard's servants of which also the Englishmen won the honour. [...]

Pseudo-Worcester

[Translated from the Latin in J. Stevenson, ed., *Letters and Papers Illustrative of the Wars of the English in France During the Reign of Henry the Sixth, King of England* (London: Longman, 1864), vol. II.2, p. 787.]

Once attributed to the fifteenth-century antiquarian, William Worcester (**) it is now accepted that this chronicle is likely a compilation of several sources, composed as one work in the sixteenth century.[146] The notice of the *emprise* is not based on first-hand accounts but is an otherwise unique, and brief abstract of the event. The style of the date suggests this comes from an ecclesiastic or cleric, with legal experience, who was comfortable rendering the 11th of June, 1467, in reference to the Church calendar of saints' days. This short passage taking note of the *emprise* is translated here from the 1864 Latin edition.

Translation

In the week of Pentecost, the Bastard of Burgundy came to England to fight a special battle with lord Anthony, Lord Scales, and other deeds, with barriers and tents at Smithfield. On the feast of St. Barnabas, having entered the place, it was said as if they were playing, and the encounters ended quickly.[147]

Hall's Chronicle

[Adapted from Edward Hall, *Hall's Chronicle [...]*. (London: Printed for J. Johnson [...], 1809), p. 268.]

Edward Hall's chronicle is a sort of proto-historical study of the period covered by the Wars of the Roses and while it has many of the genre traits of the chronicles of the period, his scholarship is sounder than one would expect from a writer who did not live through any of the events he describes. His short notice on the *emprise* of the Flower of Remembrance is included here because of his wider influence on later writers, particularly dramatists, who mined his work, more than others, for source material.

---

[146] On the spurious attribution see K. B. McFarlane, "William Worcester: A Preliminary Survey," in *Studies Presented to Sir Hilary Jenkinson*, ed. C. S. L. Davies (The Clarendon Press, 1957), pp. 196–221.

[147] The same anecdote appears in London, College of Arms, MS Arundel 5 (edited in *Three Fifteenth-Century Chronicles* p. 181) but adds a line about a recurrence of the plague.

Printed by Henry Grafton in 1548, his contemporaries were already producing historical collections covering the same period that were far less accurate and chronologically confused than this.[148] That said, Hall does compress the chronology somewhat, placing the marriage negotiations between Charles of Burgundy and Edward VI before, rather than after, the *emprise*. Hall was not the first, and certainly not the last, annalist to make this mistake. Hall also inverts the origins of the *emprise*, turning it into a challenge offered by Burgundy, and accepted by Scales. Burgundy's horse does appear, and suffer its tragic end, but Hall splits up the mounted events to separate days. The injury itself is likely derived from Fabyan. The axe combat occurs on a third day and is an embroidered version of Fabyan and others, but largely fits the historical accounts (with more editorializing). Little attention is given to the other fights and the festivities are ended by the untimely death of the Duke of Burgundy.

Transcription

But one thing was very honourable, and not meet to be put in oblivion. The Bastard of Burgundy, a man of high courage, challenged Anthony Lord Scales, brother to the Queen, a man both equal in heart and valiantness with the Bastard to fight with him both on foot and on horseback. The Lord Scales gladly received his demand and promised him on the oath of a gentleman to answer him in the field at the day appointed. Like challenges were made by other Burgundians to the gentlemen of England, which you may surely believe were not refused. The King attending to see this martial sport and valiant challenge performed, caused royal lists for the champions and costly galleries for Ladies to look on, to be newly erected and edified in West Smithfield in London. And at the day by the King assigned, the 2 Lords entered within the lists, well mounted, richly trapped, and curiously armed. On which day they ran together, certain courses with sharp spears, and so departed with equal honour. The next day they entered the field, the Bastard sitting on a bay courser, being somewhat dim of sight, and the Lord Scales had a gray courser, on whose chamfron was a long and sharp pike of steel. When these 2 valiant persons couped together at the tourney the Lord Scales horse, by chance or by custom, thrust his pike into the nostrils of the horse of the Bastard, so that

---

[148] S.T. Bindoff ed. *History of Parliament: The Commons 1509-1558* (London: Secker & Warburg, 1982), vol. II, pp. 278–82.

for very pain he mounted so high, that he fell on the one side with his master and the Lord Scales rode round about him with his sword shaking in his hand, until the King commanded the Marshall to help up the Bastard, which openly said 'I can-not hold by the clouds, for though my horse has failed me, surely I will not fail my counter-companions.' And when he was remounted, he made a countenance to assail his adversary but the King either favored his brother's honour, then gotten, or mistrusted the shame, which might come to the Bastard, if he were again foiled, caused the Heralds to cry '*a lostel*,' and every man to depart.

The morrow after, the two noble men came in to the field on foot, with two poleaxes, and there fought valiantly like two courageous champions, but at the last, the point of the ace of the Lord Scales happened to enter into the sight of the helm of the Bastard and by fine force might have plucked him on his knees, the King suddenly cast down his warder, and then the Marshals separated them. The Bastard, not content with this chance, very desirous to be revenged, trusting in his cunning at the poleaxe (the which feat he had greatly exercised and there in had a great experience) required the King of justice, that he might perform his enterprise. The Lord Scales, not refusing it. The King said he would ask council and so called to him the Constable and Marshal with the officers of arms. After long consultation had, and laws of arms rehearsed, it was declared to the Bastard for a sentence definite by the Duke of Clarence, then Constable of England, and the Duke of Norfolk, Earl Marshal, that if he would prosecute farther his attempted challenge, he must by the law of arms, be delivered to his adversary in the same case and like condition as he was when he was taken from him, that is today, the point of the Lord Scales axe to be fixed in the sight of his helm, as deep as it was when they were severed. The Bastard, hearing this judgement, doubted much the sequel, if he so should proceed again, wherefore he was content to relinquish his challenge, rather than to abide by the hazard of his dishonor. Other challenged were done and valiantly achieved by the Englishmen which I pass over. When all these courageous acts where thus with joy accomplished, the sorrowful tidings were brought to the Bastard, that Duke Phillip his father was passed this transitory life, of which tidings he was not a little sorrowful, and thereupon taking his leave of King Edward and his sister, the new Duchess of Burgundy, liberally rewarded with plate and jewels, with all celerity he returned to the new Duke Charles, his nephew [...].

BIBLIOGRAPHY

MANUSCRIPT AND ARCHIVAL SOURCES

Utrecht, Utrecht University Library, MS 1117 / Hs 6b 9

PRINTED PRIMARY SOURCES

Bentley, S., ed., *Excerpta Historica: Or Illustrations of English History* (S. Bentley, 1831).
Embree, Dan, and M. Teresa Tavormina, eds., *The Contemporary English Chronicles of the Wars of the Roses* (Boydell Press, 2019).
Fabyan, Robert, *The New Chronicles of England and France: In Two Parts*, ed. by H. Ellis (F. C. & J. Rivington; T. Payne; Wilkie and Robinson, 1811).
Gairdner, J., ed., *The Historical Collections of a Citizen of London in the Fifteenth Century*, Camden Society, New Series (Camden Society, 1876), xvii.
Gardiner, J., ed., *Three Fifteenth-Century Chronicles, With Historical Memoranda by John Stowe, the Antiquary*, Camden Society New Series (Camden Society, 1880), xxviii.
Giles, J. A., ed., 'Herne's Fragment', in *The Chronicles of the White Rose* (James Bohn, 1843), p. 18–19.
Hall, Edward, *Hall's Chronicle [...]* (Printed for J. Johnson [etc.], 1809).
Horrox, R., ed., *The Parliament Rolls of Medieval England 1275-1504 XIII: Edward IV 1461-1470*, Parliament Rolls of Medieval England (Boydell, 2005).
La Marche, Olivier de, *Mémoires d'Olivier de La Marche, maitre d'hotel et capitaine des gardes de Charles le Téméraire*, ed. by Henri Beaune and Jules d'Arbaumont (Librairie Renouard, Henri Loones, successeur, 1883).
Monstrelet, Enguerrand de, *The Chronicles of Enguerrand de Monstrelet [...] Continued by Others to the Year 1516*, ed. by Bon-Joseph Dacier and Thomas Johnes (W. Smith, 1840).
Nicolas, Harris, ed., *Proceedings and Ordinances of the Privy Council of England* (Eyre & Spottiswoode, 1837), VI.
Stow, John, *A Survey of London*, ed. by C. L. Kingsford, 2 vols. (Clarendon Press, 1908).
Thomas, A. H., and I. D. Thornley, eds., *The Great Chronicle of London* (Printed by G.W. Jones at the sign of the Dolphin, 1938).

SECONDARY SOURCES

Anglo, S., 'Financial and Heraldic Records of the English Tournament', *Journal of the Society of Archivists*, 2 no. 5 (1960), p. 183–95.
Baines, Anthony, *Woodwind Instruments and Their History*, 3rd ed. (Dover, 1991).

Baker, J. H., *An Introduction to English Legal History*, 4th ed. (Oxford University Press, 2007).
Bindoff, Stanley T., ed., *The House of Commons 1509 - 1558*, 3 vols. (Boydell & Brewer, 1982).
Boulton, D'Arcy Jonathan Dacre, *The Knights of the Crown: The Monarchical Orders of Knighthood in Later Medieval Europe; 1325-1520* (Boydell, 2000).
Brown-Grant, Rosalind, and Mario Damen, eds., *Pas d'armes and Late Medieval Chivalry: A Casebook* (Liverpool University Press, 2025).
Bühler, Curt E, 'Sir John Paston's Grete Booke, a Fifteenth-Century "Best-Seller"', *Modern Language Notes*, 56.5 (1941), p. 345–51.
Cheney, C. R., and Michael Jones, eds., *A Handbook of Dates for Students of British History*, new ed. (Cambridge University Press, 2000).
Dallas, James, 'The Bend Sinister', *Notes and Queries*, 7th series (Nov. 1887), p. 401–2.
Davies, Laura, 'Cuir Bouilli', in *Conservation of Leather and Related Materials*, ed. by Marion Kite and Roy Thomson (Elsesvier Butterworth-Heinemann, 2006), p. 94–100.
Kingsford, C. L., *Chronicles of London* (Alan Sutton, 1977).
Kohl, B., 'Tiptoft, John, 1st Earl of Worcester', *Oxford Dictionary of National Biography*, online ed. (2004).
Lester, G. A., 'Fifteenth-Century English Heraldic Narrative', *The Yearbook of English Studies*, 22 (1992), p. 201–12.
Lester, G. A., ed., *Sir John Paston's 'Grete Boke': A Descriptive Catalogue, with an Introduction, of British Library MS Landsdowne 285* (D. S. Brewer, 1984).
Lester, G. A., 'The Literary Activity of the Medieval English Heralds', *English Studies*, 71 no. 3 (1990), p. 222–29.
Lewandowski, Elizabeth J., *The Complete Costume Dictionary* (Scarecrow Press, 2011).
McFarlane, K. B., 'William Worcester: A Preliminary Survey', in *Studies Presented to Sir Hilary Jenkinson*, ed. by C. S. L. Davies (The Clarendon Press, 1957), p. 196–221).
McLaren, M-R, 'Fabyan, Robert (d.1513)', *Oxford Dictionary of National Biography*, online ed. (2004).
McLean, Will, 'Outrance and Plaisance', *Journal of Medieval Military History*, VIII (2010), p. 155–70.
Moffat, Ralph, *Medieval Arms & Armour: A Sourcebook: The Fourteenth Century. Volume 1 the Fourteenth Century*, (Boydell Press, 2022).
Moffat, Ralph, *Medieval Arms & Armour: A Sourcebook. Volume II: 1400-1450*, (Boydell Press, 2024).

Moffat, Ralph Dominic, 'The Medieval Tournament: Chivalry, Heraldry and Reality, an Edition and Analysis of Three Fifteenth-Century Tournament Manuscripts' (unpublished Ph.D., University of Leeds, 2010).

Olson, Rebecca, *Arras Hanging: The Textile That Determined Early Modern Literature and Drama* (University of Delaware Press, 2013).

Penn, Thomas, *The Brothers York: A Royal Tragedy* (Simon & Schuster, 2020).

Remnant, Mary, 'Medieval Fiddles, Etc.' *Early Music*, 5 no. 2 (1977), p. 255).

Scofield, Cora L., *The Life and Reign of Edward the Fourth, King of England and of France and Lord of Ireland*, 2 vols (Longmans, Green, 1923).

Vaughan, Richard, *Philip the Good: The Apogee of Burgundy*, New ed (Boydell Press, 2002).

Wagner, Anthony, 'Chester Herald', in *College of Arms, Queen Victoria Street*, ed. by Walter H. Godfrey, Survey of London Monograph (London Survey Committee, 1963), xvi.

CUMULATIVE BIBLIOGRAPHY

MANUSCRIPTS

Utrecht, Utrecht University Library, MS 1117 / Hs 6b 9

PUBLISHED PRIMARY SOURCES

Bentley, S., ed., *Excerpta Historica: Or Illustrations of English History* (S. Bentley, 1831).
Calendar of the Patent Rolls Preserved in the Public Record Office: Edward IV, Henry VI, A.D. 1467-1477 (Public Records Office, 1900).
Embree, Dan, and M. Teresa Tavormina, eds., *The Contemporary English Chronicles of the Wars of the Roses* (Boydell Press, 2019).
Fabyan, Robert, *The New Chronicles of England and France: In Two Parts*, ed. by H. Ellis (F. C. & J. Rivington; T. Payne; Wilkie and Robinson, 1811).
Gardiner, J., ed., *Three Fifteenth-Century Chronicles, With Historical Memoranda by John Stowe, the Antiquary*, Camden Society New Series xxviii (1880).
Giles, J.A., 'Herne's Fragment,' in J.A. Giles, ed., *The Chronicles of the White Rose*. (James Bohn, 1843).
Hall, Edward, *Hall's Chronicle [...]* (Printed for J. Johnson [etc.], 1809).
Horrox, R., ed., *The Parliament Rolls of Medieval England 1275-1504 XIII: Edward IV 1461-1470*, (Boydell, 2005).
Kingsford, C. L., ed., *Chronicles of London* (Clarendon Press, 1905).

La Marche, Olivier de, *Mémoires d'Olivier de La Marche, maitre d'hotel et capitaine des gardes de Charles le Téméraire*, ed. by Henri Beaune and Jules d'Arbaumont (Librairie Renouard, Henri Loones, successeur, 1883).
Nicolas, Harris, ed., *Proceedings and Ordinances of the Privy Council of England*, vol. VI (Eyre & Spottiswoode, 1837).
Schroeder, H. J., ed., *Disciplinary Decrees of the General Councils* (B. Herder, 1937).
Stevenson, J., ed., *Letters and Papers Illustrative of the Wars of the English in France During the Reign of Henry the Sixth, King of England*, 2 vols. in 3 parts (Longman, 1864).
Stow, John, *A Survey of London*, ed. by C. L. Kingsford, 2 vols. (Clarendon Press, 1908).
Thomas, A. H., and I. D. Thornley, eds., *The Great Chronicle of London* (Printed by G. W. Jones at the sign of the Dolphin, 1938).
Wavrin, Jehan de, *Recueil Des Chroniques et Anchiennes Istories de La Grant Bretaigne, a Present Nomme Engleterre: Volume 5, from A.D. 1447 to A.D. 1471*, ed. by William Hardy (Eyre & Spottiswoode, 1891).

SECONDARY SOURCES

Anglo, Sydney, 'Financial and Heraldic Records of the English Tournament', *Journal of the Society of Archivists*, 2, no. 5 (1960), p. 183–95.
Anglo, Sydney., 'Anglo-Burgundian Feats of Arms: Smithfield, June 1467', *Guildhall Miscellany*, 2, no. 1 (1965), p. 271–83.
———, *The Martial Arts of Renaissance Europe* (Yale University Press, 2000).
Baines, Anthony, *Woodwind Instruments and Their History*, 3rd ed. (Dover, 1991).
Baker, J. H., *An Introduction to English Legal History*, 4th ed. (Oxford University Press, 2007).
Barber, Richard, and Juliet R. V. Barker, *Tournaments* (Boydell Press, 1989).
Barker, Juliet R. V., *The Tournament in England, 1100-1400* (Boydell Press, 1986).
Bindoff, S. T., ed. *History of Parliament: The Commons 1509-1558. Volume II* (Secker & Warburg, 1982).
Boulton, D'Arcy Jonathan Dacre, *The Knights of the Crown: The Monarchical Orders of Knighthood in Later Medieval Europe; 1325 - 1520* (Boydell, 2000).
Brown, Andrew and Graeme Small, eds., *Court and Civic Society in the Burgundian Low Countries, c.1420–1530*, (Manchester University Press, 2007), p. 54–85.
Brown-Grant, Rosalind, 'Art Imitating Life Imitating Art? Representations of the Pas d'armes in Burgundian Prose Romance: The Case of Jehan d'Avennes', in *The Medieval Tournament as Spectacle: Tourneys, Jousts and Pas d'Armes, 1100-1600*, ed. by Alan V. Murray and Karen Watts (Boydell and Brewer, 2020), p. 139–54.
Brown-Grant, Rosalind, and Mario Damen, eds., *Pas d'armes and Late Medieval Chivalry: A Casebook* (Liverpool University Press, 2025).

Bühler, Curt E, 'Sir John Paston's Grete Booke, a Fifteenth-Century "Best-Seller"', *Modern Language Notes*, 56, no. 5 (1941), p. 345–51.
Burton, Danielle, *Anthony Woodville: Sophisticate or Schemer?* (Amberley, 2024).
Cheney, C. R., and Michael Jones, eds., *A Handbook of Dates for Students of British History*, new ed. (Cambridge University Press, 2000).
Dallas, James, 'The Bend Sinister', *Notes and Queries*, 7th series, (Nov. 1887), p. 401–2.
Damen, Mario, 'Tournament Culture in the Low Countries and England', in *Contact and Exchange in Later Medieval Europe Essays in Honour of Malcolm Vale*, ed. by Hannah Skoda (Boydell & Brewer, 2012), p. 247–66.
Davies, Laura, "Cuir Bouilli," in Kite, Marion, and Roy Thomson, *Conservation of Leather and Related Materials* (Elsevier Butterworth-Heinemann, 2006), p. 94–100.
Hicks, M. A, *Warwick the Kingmaker* (Blackwell, 2002).
Hicks, M. A, 'Woodville [Wydeville], Richard, First Earl Rivers (d. 1469), Magnate', *Oxford Dictionary of National Biography*, online ed. (2011).
Higginbotham, Susan, *The Woodvilles: The Wars of the Roses and England's Most Infamous Family* (The History Press, 2013).
Jones, Robert W., *Bloodied Banners: Martial Display on the Medieval Battlefield, Warfare in History* (Boydell Press, 2010).
Kaeuper, Richard W., *Holy Warriors: The Religious Ideology of Chivalry* (University of Pennsylvania Press, 2009).
Kaeuper, Richard W., and Elspeth Kennedy, *The Book of Chivalry of Geoffroi de Charny: Text, Context, and Translation.* (University of Pennsylvania Press, 1996).
Khalaf, Omar, 'Patronage, Print and the Education of the Gentry in Late Medieval England: The Case of Earl Rivers's Dicts and Sayings of the Philosophers', in *Current Issues in Medieval England*, ed. by L. Vazzosi (Peter Lang, 2021), p. 46–58.
Kingsford, C.L., *English Historical Literature in the Fifteenth Century* (Clarendon Press, 1913).
Kohl, B., 'Tiptoft, John, 1st Earl of Worcester', *Oxford Dictionary of National Biography*, online ed. (2004).
Lander, J. R., 'Marriage and Politics in the Fifteenth Century: The Nevilles and the Wydevilles', *Historical Research*, 36, no. 94 (1963), p. 119–52.
Lester, G. A., 'Fifteenth-Century English Heraldic Narrative', *The Yearbook of English Studies*, 22 (1992), p. 201–12.
Lester, G. A., ed., *Sir John Paston's 'Grete Boke': A Descriptive Catalogue, with an Introduction, of British Library MS Landsdowne 285* (D. S. Brewer, 1984).
Lester, G. A., 'The Literary Activity of the Medieval English Heralds', *English Studies*, 71, no. 3 (1990), p. 222–29.

Levitt, Emma, 'Tiltyard Friendships and Bonds of Loyalty in the Reign of Edward IV, 1461-1483', in *Loyalty to the Monarchy in Late Medieval and Early Modern Britain, c.1400-1688*, ed. by Matthew Ward and Matthew Hefferan (Palgrave, 2020), p. 1–35.

Lewandowski, E. J., *The Complete Costume Dictionary* (Scarecrow, 2011).

MacCracken, H.N., 'The Flower of Souvenance: A Moment in the Twilight of Chivalry', *The Swanee Review*, 20, no. 3 (1912), p. 366–76.

McFarlane, K. B., 'William Worcester: A Preliminary Survey', in *Studies Presented to Sir Hilary Jenkinson*, ed. by C. S. L. Davies (The Clarendon Press, 1957), p. 196–221.

McLaren, M-R, 'Fabyan, Robert (d.1513)', *Oxford Dictionary of National Biography*, Online ed. (Oxford University Press, 2004).

McLean, Will, 'Outrance and Plaisance', *Journal of Medieval Military History*, VIII (2010), p. 155–70.

Moffat, Ralph Dominic, 'The Medieval Tournament: Chivalry, Heraldry and Reality, an Edition and Analysis of Three Fifteenth-Century Tournament Manuscripts' (unpublished Ph.D., University of Leeds, 2010).

Moffat, Ralph Dominic, *Medieval Arms & Armour: A Sourcebook: The Fourteenth Century. Volume 1 the Fourteenth Century*, (The Boydell Press, 2022).

Moffat, Ralph Dominic, *Medieval Arms and Armour: A Sourcebook. Volume II: 1400-1450*, (Boydell Press, 2024).

Morgan, D., 'Herne's "Fragment" and the Long Prehistory of English Memoirs', *The English Historical Review*, 124, no. 9 (2009), p. 811–32.

Morrill, John, 'Thinking About the New British History', in *British Political Thought in History, Literature and Theory, 1500-1800*, ed. by David Armitage (Cambridge University Press, 2006), p. 23–46.

Muhlberger, Steven, 'Chivalry and Military Biography in the Later Middle Ages: The Chronicle of the Good Duke Louis of Bourbon', *The Journal of Medieval Military History*, 10 (2012), p. 114–31.

Muhlberger, Steven, *Deeds of Arms: Formal Combats in the Late Fourteenth Century* (Chivalry Bookshelf, 2005).

Nadot, Sébastien, *Le spectacle des joutes: sport et courtoisie à la fin du Moyen Âge* (Presses Universitaires de Rennes, 2012).

Nadot, Sébastien, *Rompez les lances! chevaliers et tournois au moyen âge* (Autrement, 2010).

Nievergelt, Marco, 'The Quest for Chivalry in the Waning Middle Ages: The Wanderings of René d'Anjou and Olivier de La Marche', in *Fifteenth-Century Studies 36*, ed. by Barbara I Gusick and Matthew Z. Heintzelman (Boydell and Brewer, 2011), p. 137–68.

Olson, Rebecca, *Arras Hanging: The Textile That Determined Early Modern Literature and Drama* (University of Delaware Press, 2013).

Penn, Thomas, *The Brothers York: An English Tragedy* e-book ed. (Penguin, 2020).

Pascual, Lucia Diaz, 'Jacquetta of Luxembourg, Duchess of Bedford and Lady Rivers (c. 1416-1472)', *The Ricardian*, 21 (2011), p. 67–91.
Pidgeon, Lynda, 'Antony Wydevile, Lord Scales and Earl Rivers: Family, Friends and Affinity Part 1', *The Richardian*, 15 (2005), p. 1–19.
Pidgeon, Lynda, 'Antony Wydevile, Lord Scales and Earl Rivers: Family, Friends and Affinity Part 2', *The Ricardian*, 16 (2006), p. 1–15.
Remnant, Mary, 'Medieval Fiddles, etc.' *Early Music*, 5, no. 2 (1977).
Richmond, Colin, 'Woodville [Wydeville], Anthony, Second Earl Rivers (c. 1440–1483), Magnate', *Oxford Dictionary of National Biography*, Online ed. (2011).
Ross, C. D., *Edward IV* (Yale University Press, 1997).
Ross, C. D., *Richard III* (Yale University Press, 1999).
Scofield, Cora L., *The Life and Reign of Edward the Fourth, King of England and of France and Lord of Ireland*, 2 vols (Longmans, Green, 1923).
Spencer, Dan, *Royal and Urban Gunpowder Weapons in Late Medieval England* (Boydell Press, 2019).
Vaughan, Richard, *Charles the Bold: The Last Valois Duke of Burgundy*, New ed (Boydell Press, 2002a).
Vaughan, Richard, *Philip the Good: The Apogee of Burgundy*, New ed (Boydell Press, 2002b).
Wagner, Anthony, 'Chester Herald', in *College of Arms, Queen Victoria Street*, ed. by Walter H. Godfrey, Survey of London Monograph (London Survey Committee, 1963), xvi.
Wagner, Anthony, *Heralds & Heraldry in the Middle Ages: An Inquiry into the Growth of the Armorial Function of Heralds*, 2nd ed. (Oxford University Press, 1956).

INDEX[1]

A
Anthony Woodville, Lord Scales, v, 4n15, 7, 11, 18, 19, 24, 29, 38, 46, 48, 83, 85
Antoine de Bourgogne
The Bastard of Burgundy, v, 6, 7, 7n24, 18, 26n18, 27, 27n29, 28, 46, 53–55, 78, 79, 83

B
Bastard of Burgundy, v, 7, 11, 18, 23–25, 28–31, 39, 41, 43, 46, 72–76, 78–81, 83, 84, 86, 87
Bruges, 8, 52
Brussels, 8, 24, 26, 30, 31, 43n78, 46

C
Chalon-sur-Saône, 3, 53n91
Charles, Count of Charlois

Charles the Bold, 7, 26n14
Charny, Geoffroi de, 2n1
Chester Herald, xv, 8, 9, 15–46, 16n4, 50, 60n112
Chivalry, 1

D
Duke of Bedford, 5

E
Earl of Worcester, 18, 23, 24n11, 29, 32, 34n47, 57, 59, 73
Edgecote
-battle of, 11
Edward IV, 4, 6, 6n20, 6n21, 6n23, 9, 9n32, 11, 16–18, 18n6, 33n46, 45, 58n109, 71, 77, 78, 82

---

[1] Note: Page numbers followed by 'n' refer to notes.

Emprise, vi, 2, 2n2, 4–10, 8n31, 15, 17–19, 21–26, 28–31, 38, 45–48, 49n85, 50, 51, 71, 73, 78, 79, 81–83, 86
Entrepreneur, 2, 3

G
The Great Chronicle of London, 11, 11n36

H
Henry VI, 4–6, 5n18, 11, 24n11, 36n54
Howard, Thomas, Duke of Norfolk, 10

J
Jacquetta of Luxembourg, 5, 5n17

L
Lalaing, Jacques de, 3
London, v, 9, 10, 10n35, 15, 16n4, 17, 19, 21, 23n11, 29, 31n38, 32–34, 32n41, 32n42, 36n54, 37, 37n61, 49, 50, 52, 56–60, 60n112, 60n113, 67, 72, 72n128, 74, 77–87, 86n147, 87n148
Louis XII, 4

M
Monstrelet, Enguerrand de, xv, 9, 9n33, 78–79

N
Newsells, 6, 18, 19, 38, 41

O
Olivier de La Marche, 9, 9n33, 71, 72n128

P
Pas d'armes, 2, 3, 7, 8n31, 27n28, 34n49, 72n128
Pas d'arms, vi
Pas du Compagnon a' la Larme Blanche, 7
Philip the Good, v, 4, 7, 7n24, 7n26, 26n14, 27n20, 27n23, 27n24, 27n33, 28n34, 37n58, 53n89, 72n127

R
Richard, Earl of Warwick, 5

T
Tiptoft, John, 23n11
Towton, 5, 5n18

W
Wavrin, Jehan de, 10, 53n89, 77–78
Westminster, 9, 33, 45, 58, 59, 67, 70, 71
Woodville, Anthony (Lord Scales), v, 4n15, 5, 7, 11, 18, 19, 24, 29, 38, 46, 48, 83, 85
Woodville, Elizabeth (Queen), 4–6, 5n18, 5n19, 16, 69, 69n125

9783031919091